WHEN FREEDOM CALLS

ROBERT JACKSON

ENDEAVOURINK

AN ENDEAVOUR INK PAPERBACK

First published by Arthur Barker Ltd.
in 1973

This paperback edition published in 2017
by Endeavour Ink
Endeavour Ink is an imprint of Endeavour Press Ltd
Endeavour Press, 85-87 Borough High Street,
London, SE1 1NH

ISBN 978-1-911445-93-7

Printed and bound in Great Britain by
Clays Ltd, St Ives plc

www.endeavourpress.com

Contents

Introduction   vii

1   Escape from Corregidor   3
2   The One That Got Away   21
3   Escaper Extraordinary   41
4   Farewell Campo 12   81
5   The Big Break-Out   107
6   Boldness Be My Friend   127
7   Romanian Adventure   151
8   Single to Rome   179
9   Fugitives in Siam 'Two fighters over on the
    starboard, skipper.'   211
10 I Gambled with Death – and Won   229
11 Journey to Dana   249

Acknowledgements   275

Introduction

Piecing together an anthology of escapes from wartime prison camps is not an easy task. There is, admittedly, a wealth of material to select from, and the unearthing of suitable source material presents no obstacle. The real difficulty emerges when one attempts to arrange the selected stories into a pattern, to link them together by means of a common thread.

Should they, for example, all involve successful escapes, ending happily in a 'home run'? Should they all be told in the first person? Should they all reflect the high drama that characterized some of the better-known escapes, or should some of the more trouble-free, matter-of-fact runs to freedom also be represented?

I decided to reject the idea of a 'first-person' theme throughout for one reason alone; some of the central characters in the following stories are dead. And although in one case – that of the dramatic escape of Franz von Werra – the escaper's story was told in Germany before his death, the account was heavily 'ghosted' for propaganda reasons and therefore hardly representative of the true fact. The account of the great break-out by Japanese prisoners from a camp in Australia is also presented in the third person, but for a different reason; none of the survivors who returned to Japan after the war ever told his story. Yet as the greatest PoW escape of all time, albeit ultimately unsuccessful, it fully deserves a place in this work.

One story – that of the adventures of Flight Sergeant Cyril Copley and his RAF Liberator crew, shot down over Japanese-occupied Thailand – deals, strictly speaking, with an evasion rather than an escape, but it is worthy of inclusion for its dramatic content. On the subject of successful escapes from Japanese PoW camps, I spoke to several ex-PoWs who had been prisoners in Java and Burma and asked them if they knew of any; they admitted that they did not. 'After all,' they told me, 'where was there to go if we did get away?' And, clearly, they had a point.

I also rejected the idea of selecting only those escapes which ended in 'home runs'. Several of the escapes featured in this book ended in recapture, but they were great escapes for all that, and not to have included them would have meant the loss of stories of astonishing courage and determination.

If the reader seeks a common denominator, it is therefore courage; for each of these stories displays a particular brand of courage, whether it involved the suicidal charge by a thousand Japanese against the barbed wire and machine-guns of their prison compound, the long swim by two American PoWs from Corregidor to Bataan, or the grim determination of arch-escaper Douglas Collins's ten attempts to reach freedom. For in the final analysis, it is the twin qualities of courage and determination which override all other attributes in the makeup of the persistent escaper who, ultimately, wins through to his goal.

RJ

On 7 December 1941, US Army Air Corps navigator Edgar D. Whitcomb stood by helplessly with the other crews of the 19th Bombardment Group as Japanese bombers attacked Clark Air Base in the Philippines and reduced the Group's brand-new B-17s to burning wreckage.

Whitcomb escaped from the Bataan Peninsula to Corregidor, the most heavily fortified island in the world, only to be caught up in the nightmare of the Japanese bombardment and the final ignominy of the American surrender early in May 1942. But captivity in the hands of the Japanese was not to Whitcomb's liking, and – together with Lieutenant William Harris, of the US Marines – he evolved a daring escape plan. They would swim across the long stretch of water that separated Corregidor from Bataan – and from there attempt to reach the Chinese mainland in a stolen boat . . .

1

Escape from Corregidor

The next day was 22 May 1942, and I was happier than I had been at any time since we reached Corregidor. While my fellow prisoners went about their daily routines, I was filled with excitement, for that was the day when Bill and I would make our escape from the island and from the prison camp. Neither Bill nor I made any mention to our fellow prisoners of our intention to make the swim, but about noon Bill walked over to the other side of the camp area to visit with his uncle, a lieutenant-commander in the Navy. Whether or not Bill told his uncle about his intention I never knew. In a while he was back with me, and we left our buddies and walked towards the main gate to wait for assignment on a work detail.

It was about two o'clock in the afternoon when a group of about sixty officers and men filed out of the sentry gate and made its way towards the top of the ridge to the north. Bill and I were with this group, which was headed out on a trip to gather wood for the fires back in camp. Wood was easy to find, for the trees and buildings that had been standing on Corregidor had been shattered to kindling wood by the incessant artillery fire from Bataan and the bombs from hundreds of planes that had blasted the island over the past few months. In spite of the fact that there was plenty of wood available, the men scattered over the hillside, searching as if it were hard to find. Actually, they were searching for items that might be useful back in camp – a piece of tin to cook on, an old spoon, a tin can to drink from, or just anything that could be found.

Bill and I while going through the pretence of gathering wood, wandered far to the north of the group, which was scattered far and wide over the ridge. The Jap guard was paying little attention to our activities.

'Over this way,' Bill directed as we edged farther and farther away from the group. 'There's a good place down here where we can take cover until dark.' He knew this part of the island, for it was in the area to which he had been assigned since his arrival on Corregidor a few weeks before. Nevertheless, the scenery had been so vastly changed in the last few hours of the battle that he was unable to locate the foxhole that had been so familiar to him at one time. I turned to look back at the guard, and saw that he was facing in the opposite direction from us; then, when I turned to Bill again, he was nowhere to be seen.

'Hey, Bill. Where are you?' I shouted in surprise.

'Here,' he answered, and as I looked down I found myself about to step into the hole where he was hiding.

'Quick! and be sure no one sees you.'

After another quick look towards the guard, I dropped into the hole beside Bill. It was a greater drop than I had expected, and when I looked about me I found that I was in an underground room about six feet deep, four feet wide, and ten feet long, with a small entrance at either end, just large enough for one person to climb through.

'This is the place some of the fellows dug out a few weeks ago. We should be safe here until dark. Better pull that bush back over the entrance,' he said.

The sun was still high in the western sky, and we knew that we had more than five hours to wait for darkness. The first step in our journey had been easy, and we were jubilant at our prospects for an easy escape. The inside of the cave was cool and comfortable, with no flies to torment us, and yet we could not relax. Time and again Bill and I walked to one of the entrances, stood on tiptoe, and peered out in all directions to see what we could see. After a while the wood-gatherers disappeared from the hillside, and there was nothing to be seen but the shattered ruins of the once-mighty fortress.

In the corner I found several small bottles, and upon examining them discovered that one was about half-full of quinine tablets. Into another small bottle I squeezed thirty paper dollars and sixty pesos in Philippine currency, which I had managed to keep from the Japanese, then put them in the hip pocket of my trousers with my silver wings and dog tags. We both tore our trouser legs off high above the knees, thus converting them from Army khakis to swimming shorts. Again and again we looked out over the hillside, but the scenery was always the same. At long last the sun began to sink behind the hill to the west of us; but even after that it seemed like hours before darkness descended upon Corregidor.

Although I had stood looking out across the island for several hours, waiting for the night to come, I felt a sudden apprehension when I realized that it was finally dark. The time we had been waiting for had arrived, and now it seemed that it had all happened very quickly. It seemed that it had only been a short time since we dropped into the pit, but the time had come for us to make our way down over the steep north shore and start swimming. In the sky to the east small black clouds raced across the face of the moon; but on the ground there was a quietness that was frightening. It did not seem right that at that time, one of the most important and probably the most dangerous in our lives, everything should have been so peaceful and quiet. Both of us would have been more at ease if there had been bombing and shelling; but instead, as we looked out across the island in the twilight, we saw a Corregidor that neither of us had ever seen before. There was a strange tension in the air, much like the quiet before the storm, as we tramped down over the hillside looking in every direction at once, lest a Japanese guard put a sudden end to our trip.

It was about 8.30 pm when we lowered ourselves into the water to start swimming. There I stopped for a moment to kiss the old Rock good-bye. As I hesitated before shoving off, a lot of thoughts ran through my mind. I thought of how we had made our way across the same channel in a small boat, fleeing from Bataan six long weeks before, with planes all over the sky, dive-bombing and strafing everything that moved; the new hope we had felt when we first set foot upon the fortress; the hours upon hours of sitting in a foxhole with bombs and shells falling all about and fragments of shrapnel whizzing in; the boost to the morale when we heard of the Doolittle raid on Tokyo; the empty words of encouragement from the San Francisco radio; Drachenburg, with a hole in his helmet and his head, and with shrapnel in his guts when the mortar shell had dropped between us; how we had resented not being able to fight back. We had a lot of catching up to do. 'Good-bye, Corregidor.'

'What's the matter, Ed? Something wrong?'

'No, just saying good-bye.'

It was only two or three miles across from Corregidor back to Bataan at the closest point, and it should have been possible to swim the distance in a few hours if things went well. Both Bill and I had a lot of confidence in our swimming because we had been practising every day, just off the shore from the prison camp on the opposite side of the island. We took off our shoes, socks, and shirts and lowered ourselves into the water. There was not a sign of life up or down the shore as far as we could see.

The water was cool, and it felt good to the body. We thought it would offer a kind of protection against being seen; but as I started to swim my arms glowed as if they were painted with some brilliant silver colour. I looked at Bill and could see the outline of his body with a fluorescent glow as he swam.

'What makes that glow?' I whispered.

'It's the minerals in the water. I doubt if we can be seen very far away,' was the response. But even with that assurance I swam so that I made a minimum of disturbance in the water, and kept looking back towards the shore for any possible signs of life.

After about half an hour we appeared to be a considerable distance from the shore; however, the dark outline of the Bataan coast ahead seemed very little closer to us.

'How're you going?' Bill asked.

'Fine. This is great. The way I feel, I could swim all night.'

'I think we ought to swim for that light, the brighter one of the two,' Bill suggested.

'I've been watching it, and I believe we're getting closer to it all the time. At least it's looking brighter to me,' I said.

Off to our right and in a north-easterly direction a big black cloud seemed to hang over Manila Bay. The cloud seemed to grow darker as we swam. As I looked at it, Bill said, 'Hope that big cloud over there stays where it is until we get to Bataan.'

'Oh, I don't think we have anything to worry about. At the rate we're travelling, we should be there before the cloud gets here even if it is coming in our direction.'

'Sure, look back there. We're really leaving old Corregidor in our past,' Bill assured me. After that we swam for a long time without talking. It seemed to be too good to be true we were on our way to freedom. All we had to do was to keep swimming towards that little light on the Bataan coast. Several times I convinced myself that we were close to it and it looked much brighter; but then again it would look just as dim as it had looked when we had first started our swim.

After a long while it started to sprinkle lightly, and the water was not as smooth as it had been before. 'Looks like we're in for a little shower,' Bill observed.

'Yes, I felt some drops, and it looks like that cloud

is beginning to reach us.' As if in answer to my state-ment, it started raining a little harder.

'Still see the light?' he asked.

'Sometimes it seems to fade out for a while, but then it comes back again. I'm sure we're still headed in the right direction,' I answered.

Again we lapsed into silence and settled down to the business of swimming. There could be no question that we were getting closer to the shore. I thought of what a wonderful thing that would be. We could walk to Cabcaben Field and find some of the Filipinos and get something to eat. Then we could sleep in the jungles, far away from all the things we had been doing during the past few weeks. As I swam along I cupped my hand to my lips to catch a few drops of the fresh water that was coming down more heavily. I managed to get a few drops before a big wave swept over me and choked me as it forced salt water into my throat and nose. I coughed and tried to get my breath. I called for Bill to hold up for a minute. Then I realized that I had not been in contact with Bill for a long time. I looked all about me, only to find that the waves had grown higher, and it was impossible to see more than a few feet in any direction.

'Hey, Bill!' I screamed at the top of my voice. No answer. 'Hey, Bill! Where are you?' I shouted it again and again, trying to rise as high in the water as I could to look about me. The wind was blowing, rain was coming down in torrents, and the waves were breaking over my head even though I did everything possible to keep it above the water. The terrible thought struck me that something had happened to Bill. He was lost, and I was alone in the middle of the North Channel. I trod water and shouted until I was certain that he would never answer. Then I realized for the first time what a foolish idea this swim had been, and I understood why the others back in camp had ridiculed the idea of swimming to the mainland to escape.

I remembered how some of them had said, 'Let's wait until we get to the mainland before we try to escape.' I remembered some of their discussions about the strong current in the channel and about the sharks. I also remembered Bill when he had said, 'You don't want to spend another day in this hell, do you?' That was why we had been so impatient. That was why we had been willing to take the chance, because we felt that we would surely die if we remained there.

Again I tried, 'Bill, for Christ's sake, where are you? Answer me!' Then I thought I heard a sound above the roar of the water.

'That you, Bill? Answer again. I think I heard you,' I shouted, trying desperately to swim in the direction from which the sound came. I suddenly realized I was making no progress. Although I was trying hard, I was bobbing like a cork in the big waves. Then I heard, 'Ed!'

'Yeah, Bill. I hear you! I hear you!' I shouted, and I thought I saw a dark figure ahead. 'For Christ's sake, Bill, let's don't get lost again,' I pleaded.

'We'd better check with each other and talk to each other more,' he suggested. 'Wonder where we are. Haven't seen the light for some time.'

'Neither have I,' I answered. 'I've been looking for you.'

We talked, bobbing up and down with one big wave after another. There was no use in trying to swim, for we could make no headway, and we had not the slightest idea in which direction to proceed. We had been in the water at least three or four hours and should have been near the Bataan coast; but the sky was black and the sea was black. There was nothing for us to do but tread water, wait until the storm subsided, and keep from getting separated.

It was a long time before the rain began to slacken, but even before it had stopped completely, we were again able to see a tiny light shining in the distance.

'There it is,' Bill said, and we both started swimming again with new enthusiasm.

Bill said, in a very discouraged voice, 'I'm afraid it's a star, Ed. Looks too high in the sky to be a light.'

It was still rather faint, but I strained my eyes harder and harder. 'It may be. No, wait a minute; it is a light, and it's not very far away. I think I can see the shore right over there.'

'Yeah, that's it!' Bill saw it too.

Our luck had changed. At the time when we had been bobbing up and down in the big waves of the channel thinking we were hopelessly lost, we were just off the shore of Bataan. We were very close to the shore, and all we had to do was to get in to land without being seen by the Japs. The light was probably an enemy encampment.

Through the mist something big loomed up ahead of me. 'Looks like a big wall up there, Bill.'

'Wall, nothing,' Bill whispered in alarm. 'That's a ship. Let's get out of here before they see us.'

We turned and swam in the other direction for a considerable distance before we stopped and looked back. By that time the atmosphere had cleared, and we were able to make out the outline of a large transport near a dock.

'Can you make that out?' I asked, because it did not look familiar to me.

'Looks like the North Mine Dock to me,' Bill said meekly.

'Couldn't be,' I replied, but even as I spoke, I recognized the pier and big Malinta Hill behind it. 'Well, I'll be damned. Let's get away from here.'

There was no question that it was the North Mine Dock of Corregidor, and we were only about a hundred yards from the shore and not more than half a mile from the place where we had started swimming several hours before. The storm and the current had played tricks on us and swept us back down the coast. After several hours of swimming and battling the waves we were no nearer to Bataan than we had been when we started. We could see no signs of life on the ship, but we kept swimming away from it.

'Think we can still make it before daylight?' I asked.

'Don't know. It's worth a try. There's no turning back now. Better to try anything than to go back to Corregidor,' came the answer.

Bill was right. Anything was better than that – even the bottom of the sea. By now the water was smooth again, and swimming was easy. The night cleared up beautifully; and after a while the clouds above began to break up so that we could again see the stars. We could easily see each other, so we swam on for a long time without a word between us. There was nothing to say. We had a long swim before us.

Swimming sidestroke, I would reach out with my right hand far in front of me, pull an arm full of water back past my body, then kick. Then there was a small stroke with my left hand while the right reached out again. It was pull, kick, pull, kick, on and on, mechanically, like walking hour after hour. For a long time it seemed that we were suspended there between the two shores, getting neither nearer to Bataan nor farther from Corregidor.

'What if it gets light and we're still out here swimming?'

and without waiting for an answer to my question, I went on, 'We might possibly make it to shore without being seen, even in the daytime.'

How long those thoughts ran through my mind, I had no idea. It was like a dream, being somewhere and not being able to get away; but I was suddenly brought out of my bad dream when something hit my leg. Then it hit me again. Was it a shark? 'Bill!' I screamed.

'What is it?' he asked in alarm.

'Nothing,' I answered shortly. I could see no point in telling him and having him as frightened as I was at that moment. I imagined I saw fins cutting the water in circles about me, and at any moment I expected to be hit again. The next time I was hit, it was only a light touch.

Then Bill spoke up. 'I think little fish are trying to eat me alive.'

That was it! It was little fish. They were swimming along, trying to nibble at my arms and legs. After a while they left us, and all was calm again.

By this time it was clear that we were getting closer and closer to shore; then old Venus came peeking up over the eastern horizon like the red light that pops up on the instrument panel of a plane, saying 'Fuel pressure is getting low'. Old Venus seemed to be a warning light to us. We started swimming faster and faster, for it was beginning to get light.

Off to our right we were able to make out an object which we were unable to identify.

'Is that a ship?' I asked.

'Seems to be standing still, whatever it is.' We strained our eyes at the object until it took the form of a large sea-going barge.

'It's not too far away,' I observed.

'No, I don't think so. Maybe we had better go over and spend the day on her rather than try to make it to shore,' Bill suggested.

We changed our course slightly to the right in order to bring ourselves closer to the barge. We were both very tired and eager to get some rest. But before we were half-way to the barge, we were able to make out the trees on the shoreline more distinctly, and we could see that it was only a short distance from us. Without a word we turned and headed for the shore, which offered much better security for us than the Japanese barge.

Some twenty feet before we reached the shore we came upon a lot of large rocks, and like two monsters emerging from the water, we struggled our way across the rocks and on to the shore. The place appeared to be completely deserted.

It was not until we were on solid ground that we realized how completely exhausted we were. In the cold grey dawn of Bataan I turned and had one last look across the channel, back to Corregidor. Then we both dropped exhausted into a clump of bushes.

When we awoke, the sun was low in the western sky. We were free!

*

Unfortunately, their freedom was short-lived. Both were recaptured after spending several weeks on the run, sheltered by friendly Filipinos and hunted by the Japanese. Whitcomb posed as an American mining engineer and was imprisoned in a civilian internment camp; his ruse held good and he was repatriated to the USA with a batch of civilians in 1943 – Bill Harris was not so lucky. He spent the rest of the war in a prison camp near Tokyo. He was killed in Korea in 1950 during the US Marines' 'fighting retreat' to Hagaru before the Chinese Communists.

Of the thousands of German soldiers, sailors and airmen captured during the Second World War, only one – Oberleutnant Franz von Werra, a Luftwaffe fighter pilot – succeeded in making a 'home run' from Allied territory.

Captured when his Messerschmitt 109 was shot down over southern England during the Battle of Britain, von Werra made a succession of abortive escapes from prison camps in England – including one that came perilously close to succeeding when he tried to steal a Hurricane fighter from an RAF base.

Early in 1941, von Werra was transferred to Canada – and it was there, from a PoW train travelling close to the border of the still neutral USA, that he made his final bid for freedom.

2

The One That Got Away

Von Werra landed on piled snow at the side of the track. The force of the impact drove all the breath from his body. He lay for a minute, feeling sick from the shock. He had ricked his neck in the fall, and he ached all over.

He stood up dizzily and looked around him. The cold struck him like a blow – he had jumped from stifling heat into thirty degrees of frost. The perspiration congealed on his skin.

There was snow everywhere, the smell of pine trees. In the distance, a red pin-point of light. The train's rear lamp. Then it was gone.

He felt a sudden surge of exhilaration.

His temples throbbed, his neck ached, he was stiff, chilled to the marrow, and his nose stung like hell. But he was free.

He became aware of the silence – the silence of snow. It was as though his ears were plugged with cotton wool.

The sky was clear and the stars hung low and large. The snow reflected their diamond light.

Heavens, it was cold!

What a fool he had been not to think of getting a cap. He would have to do something or his ears would drop off with frostbite. He pulled from his pocket the tartan scarf he had bought at Swanwick, and wrapped it over his head.

Having taken a bearing on the pole star, he crossed the railway track and set out southwards across a stretch of open country. The going was difficult. Each step he took he sank up to his calves in snow. The harsh, rasping sound of his boots in the snow seemed to fill the universe.

He began to imagine noises, and when he glanced back quickly over his shoulder, it was not only to check his bearing by the pole star.

After about an hour he saw the serrated outline of a pine forest, black against the pale horizon. There was no road or track along the edge of it. There was nothing for it but to find his way through.

The forest was full of noises – creaking, scufflings, whisperings, sighings, rustlings – breaking the awesome silence.

Sometimes he was in the open, knee-deep in snow, sometimes groping, stumbling in the blackness under the trees. After a while he came to a broad avenue. It was a hundred yards wide – probably a fire break. The snow in the middle had been flattened by a tractor. It was like walking on a road. Ahead of him the tree-tops formed an elongated V against the stars. Behind him the sky was paling. Dawn was near.

He hurried. The hard track was a godsend, but he was afraid that as soon as it became daylight he might encounter lumberjacks, or perhaps the man with the tractor. How could he explain his presence in the middle of a Canadian forest in such clothes at that time of day? He must get on to a highway.

The sun rose. The tips of the trees on his right were edged with gold and silver. The pines cast gigantic shadows. He hastened onwards, sometimes running. He was reluctant to leave the hard track.

He must have walked several miles, but still the end of the avenue was not in sight. Suddenly he heard the sound of an engine. It sounded like a car, and it seemed to come from the trees on his right. He listened intently. The noise grew louder, and after a few moments a car flashed across the avenue half a mile away ahead of him, snow-chains rattling.

A road; in a few minutes he had reached it.

For an hour he followed it without seeing any more vehicles. Then it joined a wider road. There was a signpost.

*

According to the announcement put out by the Canadian authorities, von Werra escaped from the train near Smiths Falls, Ontario, about forty miles south-west of Ottawa. If that was so, he had only about thirty miles to cover to reach the St Lawrence, which at that point forms the border between Canada and the United States.

When eventually he reached New York and was besieged by reporters, sensing the sort of story they were after, he gave it to them. He said he had leapt off the train 100 miles north of Ottawa; this gave him far more elbow room for an extravagant account in the true von Werra manner, of his achievement and of the daring and aplomb with which he had brought it off. No one enjoyed more than von Werra telling a good story for the entertainment of his audience, and if their legs were pulled in the process, so much the better!

His story having been accepted by the American Press (who after all would have no means of knowing the real route taken by the prisoners' train and presumably did not bother to discover for themselves that no east-west rail-track passes within a hundred miles of 'a hundred miles north of Ottawa'), there seemed to von Werra no reason to vary his account when he came to write it in book form for the German people. Indeed he improved on it.

First of all a truck had come along and he had

thumbed a lift in the manner Wagner* had taught him. He had a story ready for the driver. He was a Dutch seaman. He had been twice dive-bombed crossing the Atlantic and had seen too many ships sunk by U-boats. He had had enough. He had relatives in Ottawa who would help him get a land job.

After some miles the lorry driver set von Werra down where he was due to turn off the main highway. 'Plenty of stuff heading for Ottawa on this route,' had been the driver's parting remark. 'You'll soon hitch a ride, bud.'

Sure enough after a quarter of a mile, von Werra had heard a rattle of snow-chains coming behind him. He removed his hand from his pocket ready to carry out the Wagner drill again. When he looked back his heart missed a beat. He quickly put his hand back into his pocket and turned his back on the approaching vehicle. It was a big saloon car. On its bumper there was a large red shield bearing the word 'POLICE'.

Von Werra pretended to ignore the car as it drew level, but the driver braked and pulled in beside him.

So his third attempt had not been lucky after all. Had he been a fool to walk along the main highway instead of keeping to the forest where he would have been safe?

The policeman was beckoning to him to get in. He

*a companion in prison camp

25

had no option. Inside he noticed the radio receiver. That explained it. Police cars were probably out scouring every highway looking for a short, fair man wearing a blue overcoat and no hat.

But from the policeman's opening remarks it appeared that he was more concerned with von Werra's half complete hitchhiking gesture. What Wagner had been unable to tell him was that since the beginning of the war begging a lift had been made illegal in Canada. 'You changed your mind just in time,' the policeman had said. 'If you'd hailed me, I'd have had to run you in. As it is I'll run you into Ottawa.' For von Werra had told him about his 'relatives' in Ottawa.

Whether any policeman ever did help von Werra on his way we are unlikely to know. If the policeman did not exist, at least he could not come forward to contradict von Werra's story! If, as von Werra said, the policeman dropped him off outside police head-quarters, it was certainly not in Ottawa, where he also placed some other daring adventures. He had gone into one of the big banks and asked to change English currency into Canadian dollars; he had not revealed that all he had to exchange was a ten-shilling note. When the clerk behind the grille had demanded to see his papers, von Werra had once more escaped from a desperate situation. He had another story for American newspaper men, that he had narrowly escaped arrest by police guarding the Parliament Building while he was sightseeing in the capital; but this one he must have forgotten by the time he came to dictate notes for his book.

If, as the Canadian authorities stated, and as his companion, Wagner, confirms, von Werra left the train near Smiths Falls, he certainly never went near Ottawa, which lay in the opposite direction – i.e. northwards – to that in which he wanted to go.

What his object can have been in making up such a tale, is left to the imagination of the reader, who has already had experience of von Werra's gift for extemporizing.

One incident must have had some truth in it, for von Werra describes a ruse by which he acquired a road map from a garage, and an 'Imperial' road map of Ontario State was among the items later found in his possession.

The indisputable fact remains that in due course, from whichever direction and by whatever means, von Werra did arrive in Johnstown on the north bank of the St Lawrence and saw the twinkling lights of the United States beckoning him from the other shore.

He had no idea how he was going to cross the river. According to his map, there were international bridges at Cornwall, forty-five miles downstream, and at Thousand Islands, forty miles upstream. Between the two bridges, there were ferries at Morris-burg, Prescott and Brockville. Prescott was the nearest, only a few miles away, and he decided to investigate that first. But would the ferry be working at that time of year? It seemed unlikely in view of the ice he had seen on the river from the train, farther downstream between Quebec and Montreal.

He walked south and came to what appeared in the gathering dusk to be a wide, flat snow-covered valley. It was a few seconds before he realized that this was the River St Lawrence. It was frozen over. He was tremendously excited. All he had to do was to wait until it was quite dark and walk across to the United States. It was far better than a ferry or toll bridge where he would have to run the gauntlet of customs, passport officials and police of two countries.

But the size of the river was terrifying. How wide was it? Five hundred metres? A thousand? The dusk and the snow made it impossible to judge. But it was a long, long way to the winking lights of the American city on the other side, which he reckoned from his map to be Ogdensburg.

He set out along the bank, wading knee-deep through the snow. He was dead tired and ravenously hungry. He had eaten nothing for nearly twenty-four hours. It had been cold enough all day, but with the approach of night the temperature dropped rapidly. There was a bitter wind at his back. It pierced his clothing like a knife. The cold and fatigue had made him drowsy. He fretted with impatience.

He had travelled so far; now there was only three-quarters of a mile at the most between him and final freedom.

He struggled for about two miles along the bank. It was desolate and silent. There was only the hum of the wind round his ears, the occasional flurries of powder blown along the surface of the snow.

He waited until long after dark. A haze of light hung over Ogdensburg. Some distance to the east of it there were three isolated points of light forming a triangle. Perhaps they were street lamps. He made them his objective.

At seven o'clock he left the comparative shelter of the bank and set off across the open ice of the river.

The snow had been blown into deep drifts near the bank. He floundered, fought his way forward foot by foot. Fifty yards out the going became comparatively easy, but the wind swept over the ice straight up the course of the river. It seemed to be laden with splinters of glass. Ice formed on his eyebrows, on the scarf over his head and on the upper part of his coat. Snow from the drifts he had struggled through turned to ice as he walked; the flaps of his coat were like boards.

The glittering stars and the lights of Ogdensburg merged and traced scintillating lines across the snow. The merging of land and sky gave him the illusion that he was about to look over the edge of the world. The illusion vanished as the lights of the city ahead became more distinct.

Now and again he heard the sound of the ice cracking – a sharp snap followed by a rapidly receding rumble. He knew that cracking ice was not dangerous so long as it was freezing. But when he reached what he thought was about half-way, the sounds of cracking became very loud and menacing. Sometimes they were close and he could feel the sudden shock wave. An odd sensation.

He tripped over something and went sprawling. The ice was no longer smooth under its thin covering of snow, but jagged and rough as a road surface broken up by a pneumatic drill. He was so numb from cold that it was a minute or so before he felt the full hurt of his tumble.

He was winded and shaken. He lay for a moment, almost overcome by the urge to sleep, his senses pulling one way, his will the other. There came to his mind the memory of a summer evening on a lake near Berlin: green reeds rustling, sun-spangled water, white sails billowing, ripples lapping against glistening, varnished woodwork. Lapping . . . lapping . . .

The wind dropped momentarily and he clearly heard the sound of a car horn. He got up, aching all over, slipping and stumbling on slabs of ice larger than paving stones. He was only a quarter of a mile from the American shore. Cars rolled along the waterfront, head-lights blazing.

He hurried forward eagerly, then paused. Ten, fifteen yards ahead the snow seemed to stop. Beyond was blackness. The shore already? But why was there no snow?

Then he saw the lights reflected on the blackness: water! He could not grasp it. How could there be water when the whole river was frozen over? He frantically hacked with the heel of his boot at a slab of ice. A corner broke off and he tossed it forward into the blackness. It fell with a hollow splash, like a pebble into a well.

There was an ice-free channel between him and the American shore.

To swim in that temperature meant certain death. He had to go back.

Von Werra returned to the Canadian bank and walked along it towards Prescott. He came to a collection of chalets – a deserted summer holiday camp. He floundered about in the deep snow on the foreshore and eventually found what he was looking for – a long, cigar-shaped mound of snow. He scraped away the side with his boot and came upon something hard. It was an upturned rowing boat.

He went back to the chalets and found a wooden fence. After much kicking and wrenching he managed to free two palings. They were too wide and too thick and ice made them heavier still, but they would have to do. He used one of them as a shovel to dig away the snow from the boat.

It was a large, cumbersome affair, and was frozen to the ground. He had to lever it free, a little at a time, with one board, using the other as a wedge. When he had freed it he still had to turn it the right way up. It took all his strength and the aid of the two boards but finally he righted it.

There were no oars or rowlocks. The boat was a six-seater. However was he going to row it – even assuming he could manage to drag it as far as the water?

He groped around, looking for another boat. He found nothing, so returned to the six-seater.

He had got to do it!

In a sudden, desperate rage, he threw himself at the stern of the boat and pushed wildly. It scarcely moved.

He felt a snowflake on his cheek. He looked up at the sky. The stars were obscured. He looked across the river. The lights of Ogdensburg were barely discernible through a curtain of flurrying snow.

It would be fatal to give way to rage and panic. He must conserve his strength, use his wits to spare his muscles, and make every scrap of effort count.

If he tried to drag the boat, he would waste a lot of effort, for he would tend to pull the bow down into the snow. He must push it. When he got out beyond the drifts, where the snow was only ankle deep on the ice, he could tie his scarf to the mooring ring in the bow and pull the boat behind him.

He tossed the boards into the boat and began pushing

it towards the river. He advanced a foot to eighteen inches at a time. At first he thought he would never reach the river. But gradually he stopped thinking. He became an automaton, oblivious to everything except the rhythm of his movements, the rasping of his breath and the taste of his saliva. Fatigue, hunger, thirst and cold were forgotten.

At last he reached the open ice. He crouched down on the lee of the boat out of the wind and the driving snow, resting. When he got up again and tried to push, the keel was frozen to the ice. He had to wrench with all his might to free it. It was wasted effort – he must not rest any more until he reached the pack-ice.

He tried to tie his scarf to the mooring ring, but his fingers were without feeling and for the life of him he could not tie a knot. He would have to continue pushing.

Half-way across.

Sometimes for minutes at a time the lights of Ogdensburg were completely obscured by snow. Von Werra kept pushing. He dared not stop. Now and again he slipped and fell on to his knees. But he got up and went on.

He was brought to a halt by the pack-ice near the water's edge. How could he get the boat over the ice and into the river?

He pulled the boat back a few feet, then pushed it up on to the pack-ice using the two boards as runners under the keel. Again, using the boards alternately as runners, he managed to push the boat forward, a length at a time.

At last he reached the open river. He tipped the boat three-parts of the way into the water, jumped in and pushed off against the ice with one of the boards. The whole boat slid into the water, rocked violently and in the struggle to regain his balance the board slipped out of his numbed hand.

He sat down and picked up the remaining board, trying to use it as a paddle. But it was too long, too heavy and too clumsy. He could neither feel it nor grip it. It slid out of his hands into the water.

Rudderless, oarless, the boat floated away into the darkness, rocking and turning lazily round and round in the ten-miles-an-hour current. Now and again small icefloes thudded against the sides.

An escaper must have luck. Farther downstream the ice-free channel followed the contour of a toe of land jutting out into the river. The boat, steadied now and facing upstream, gradually slid across the channel and eventually bumped and scraped along the jagged ice bordering one side of the headland.

Von Werra was no stranger to excitement. But even he found the thrill of that trip on the St Lawrence a little too hectic and sustained. Time seemed to stop. He had the impression that the boat was spinning round and round in the darkness, and hurtling down to the sea.

When it bumped and grated against the margin of ice by the headland, he needed no time to make up his mind. The boat grated: he leapt. He managed to fall on the ice. The boat recoiled, then slowly returned. The last he heard of it, it was bumping and scraping slowly downstream.

He got to his feet, staggered across the ice and scrambled up the bank. He was very anxious. It seemed to him that he had been in the boat for hours, and that he had drifted miles. And he knew from the map that farther downstream the USA border was some way south of the St Lawrence – that both banks were in Canada.

He saw a huge building some distance away on his left. The windows were ablaze with light. Then he had a shock. He noticed that every window was barred. Had he landed in the grounds of a penitentiary?

He moved away to the right as quickly as he could. He was reassured when he saw a car pass by ahead of him. There must be a road. Then he saw two cars parked farther down on the right. He got on to the road and walked towards them. The leading car was unoccupied. The bonnet of the other was raised and a man was tinkering with the engine. A young lady in a snow-sprinkled fur coat stood by him and there was another girl sitting in the car.

On the licence plate of the rear car were the words: 'New York'. It was the same with the other car. He dared not believe it. He had seen cars in Canada with New York licence plates.

The man went to the car ahead, presumably to get

some tools. He looked hard at von Werra but did not speak.

Von Werra moved across the front of the car. The headlamps shone on his overcoat, which was stiff with ice. His legs cast long shadows on the snow. The woman stared at him and then glanced in the direction of the river from which he had come. She laughed and asked lightly:

'What's the matter with you?'

'Excuse me. Is this America?'

'Are you sick or something?'

'No, truly. What is that house over there? What place is this?'

The woman was struck by his accent and by the tiredness of his voice. She replied straightforwardly:

'That is New York State Hospital. I am a nurse there. You are in Ogdensburg.'

'Ogdensburg? But . . . ' Von Werra could not believe it.

Instead of having drifted miles downstream, he had travelled barely half a mile.

But what did it matter? He was in America.

He smiled wearily.

'I am an officer of the German Air Force,' he said 'I escape across the river from Canada. I am – ' he corrected himself – 'I was a prisoner of war.'

*

Von Werra was lucky; other German prisoners who later tried to follow his example were arrested by the US authorities and handed back to the Canadians.

Regaining Germany by way of Mexico, South America, Africa, Spain and Italy, it was not long before he was once more flying operationally with a fighter squadron assigned to coastal defence and based in Holland.

On 25 October 1941, the luck that had been von Werra's companion for so long finally deserted him. During a patrol along the coast, the engine of his Messerschmitt *failed and it dived into the sea.*

No trace of either aircraft or pilot was ever found.

Without doubt, Flight Lieutenant Allan F. McSweyn, an Australian pilot serving with No 115 Squadron RAF, can lay claim to have been one of the most persistent escapers on record. Shot down during his twenty-fifth mission over Germany in July 1941, he was placed in one German prison camp after another – and escaped from them all, on one occasion attempting to steal a Messerschmitt *110. This is his remarkable story, culminating in his final and successful escape bid that took him across the breadth of Germany, through France and eventually to Spain.*

3

Escaper Extraordinary

Would I be able to steal a *Messerschmitt* 110? I anxiously pondered this difficult problem as I crouched in the German wheatfield in which I was hiding on the edge of a *Luftwaffe* night-fighter airfield. As I lay there concealed, throughout the summer day, I could make out through the wheat stalks the busy forms of German mechanics working on aircraft. At about six o'clock, a *Messerschmitt* 110 that was only about 100 yards away from my hiding-place was refuelled, rearmed – and generally prepared for night flying. I made up my mind to try to fly that *Messerschmitt* back to England. However, because of roving patrols, I decided to wait till dark before I made my desperate attempt.

The date was the beginning of July 1941. A night or two earlier, my Wellington 1C had been shot down after I had bombed Bremen. I was an Australian pilot who had been operating with No 115 Squadron from Marham – and I had had to bale out on this twenty-fifth op. So far, I had managed to evade capture – and I had been making towards the Dutch or Belgian borders, hoping to link up with local patriots and so get back home, when I had found myself near this *Luftwaffe* night-fighter base. Now, as darkness fell, I crept cautiously out of my hiding-place – and stealthily made my way towards the nearby *Messerschmitt* 110.

The cockpit canopy was open, I noticed, as I got near the dark hulk of the German night-fighter. Quickly, I glanced around to make sure that no one was watching. Then, my heart pounding, I clambered aboard the aircraft. The cockpit layout, I saw at once, was completely different from that of any other machine I had ever flown. However, I quickly got the hang of the basic controls, and, after a few minutes, I felt sufficiently at home to believe that I stood a good chance of taking off – and of getting the *Messerschmitt* back to England in one piece. Thinking quickly, I made a shrewd guess at the starting procedure. Then I turned on the petrol, set my throttles, gave a short prayer – and pressed the starter button.

The initial result was not too bad – for the port engine at least started to turn over. However, I was quite unable to get it to fire, no matter what I did. I did not want to waste the aircraft batteries completely, so I took another thorough look around the cockpit.

Meanwhile, I hoped that no one would come over to the aircraft.

Suddenly, however, I was horrified to see one of the guards come across to the machine and look up at the cockpit. In sheer desperation, I pressed the starter button again, hoping that I would be able to get the engine to start before I was ignominiously hauled out of the cockpit. However, to my astonishment, the ground-staff man walked underneath the port engine, fiddled around under the cowling for a few seconds – then called out something. I thought he was probably helping me to start the engine and wanted me to have another go. So I pressed the starter button.

The German was obviously shattered by this action, for the propeller nearly knocked his head off. Not surprisingly, he came round to the cockpit to see what was going on. When he looked up, I do not know which of us was the more astonished: for, instead of finding a smartly turned-out young *Luftwaffe* pilot sitting in the cockpit, he was faced by a rather grubby – and certainly nervous – Australian.

The German erk was so shocked that he practically fell backwards off the wing. Immediately, he yelled loudly for help. Then he came towards the cockpit pointing an extremely businesslike-looking rifle straight at me. A few moments later, several guards came running to the mechanic's aid. I had no alternative, of course, but to surrender, and was hauled off to the German equivalent of the guardroom.

After a series of interrogations, I was later taken to a succession of PoW camps. But, from the moment I was captured, one thought constantly dominated my mind: I was determined to escape.

The most spectacular of the early escape attempts in which I was involved was a mass attempt to scale the wire around the camp with extension ladders. On the selected night, all the lights in the camp were fused by an electrically-minded prisoner, and a row was created elsewhere to divert the attention of the sentries. Then we escapers, in three teams of twenty each, placed our ladders, built from bed boards and sides of beds, against the fence. Afterward, the extension part was raised to cover the eight feet or so between the inner and outer wires. We then scaled the ladders, crossed the wires, dropped to the ground, and tried to escape under cover of darkness. Quite a number of men managed to get away in the ensuing panic, and three Army officers did, in fact, get back to England as a result of this escape. However, the rest of us were fairly quickly rounded up and returned to camp.

But I was still determined to get out; and, during the fifteen months I spent at Warburg, I was personally interested in about four separate escape attempts. Three of these attempts were tunnels, in which we had little luck, since each of them was found before completion.

The fourth attempt was an endeavour to escape in the back of a bread cart. I managed to get out of the camp by hiding in the cart when it was on its way back to the local village after delivering our bread. But unfortunately, I was stopped by two German soldiers who saw me crossing a paddock. I attracted their attention because I was dressed in reasonably good civilian clothes and the circumstances were obviously unusual. Since I could not speak the language very well and could not give them a satisfactory explanation as to my presence in the area, I was taken back to the camp for questioning. I received the usual seven days solitary confinement.

When I was transferred to *Oflag* 21B at Schubin, escape attempts came fast and furious. With several others, I concocted a scheme to dig a tunnel out – but unfortunately, our tunnel was discovered by the Germans. A plan to escape by mounting extension ladders against the wire, as we had done at Warburg, was also wrecked. Afterwards, I had a narrow escape, when trying to cut my way through the wires surrounding the camp, to get away under cover of darkness. I teamed up with a fellow-Australian named Tom Gilderthorpe to try to pull off this attempt. We began the attempt on two or three occasions, but always something stopped us getting to the wire. The night we finally made our bid for freedom occurred shortly after a warning had been issued that anyone caught trying to escape would be shot on sight. This threat hanging over our heads did not help to boost our morale as we wormed our way across the trip wire placed ten feet back from the main wires, and beyond which no prisoner could step without being shot at. We could work uninterrupted on cutting the wire for periods of only about two minutes before we had to knock off to lie perfectly still while the sentry passed within a few feet of where we were operating. Obviously, it was not possible to make any quick movements or noise without fear of detection.

Since I could not check accurately on the movements of the sentry patrolling outside the fence, we rigged up a warning system. Tom lay in a vegetable patch, holding a piece of string attached to my right foot – and signalled when the coast was clear for me to resume cutting. However, progress was slow; and it soon became apparent that we would not be able to cut through the full set of wires in the limited time available.

Our minds were finally made up for us when the sentry noticed my presence in the wire. Rather than wait to be arrested, Tom and I decided to risk a wild dash back to our quarters. Separating, we ran as fast as we could – zigzagging to reduce the chance of being shot. The sentry fired only one shot – and, fortunately, this came nowhere near us. When we got back to camp, we were able to hide our provisions and escape equipment before the Germans arrived to carry out a search. They found nothing.

*

Meanwhile, we had been working on a tunnel, planning to break from it in the spring of 1943. But, just as our tunnel was ready to be broken, the Germans smelt a rat – and imposed many additional anti-escape precautions. Consequently, it was decided to put off our escape attempt for a couple of weeks. At this stage, I heard that we were to be moved yet again – this time to *Stalag Luft* 3 at Sagan. Taking all the circumstances into account, I decided that I would stand the best chance of escape if I made my attempt from Sagan. Puzzling over the best method to adopt, I finally decided to switch identities with one of the orderlies in Schubin, my present camp – in an endeavour to enter Sagan as an orderly.

The main reason why I decided to exchange identities was that it was much easier for an orderly to escape than an officer. Normally, an officer was not allowed out of camp. However, orderlies and NCOs attached to officers' camps for camp duties were regularly required to leave the camp boundaries to collect bread, coal and German food rations. Orderlies even had the opportunity of getting outside the camp – and, although they were always under German guard, they had far less attention paid to them than would be paid to officers. In addition, if I completed my exchange of identities successfully, I stood a chance of being able to get myself transferred to a troops' camp – from which escape would be much easier.

At this stage, I met Private John McDiarmid, of the Seaforth Highlanders. McDiarmid was an orderly in our barracks. He was roughly my own build, though a little taller; but he was not so unlike me that a rather blurred photograph could not be mistaken for either of us. To my delight, when I approached him, I found him quite happy to exchange identities before we left Schubin. However, because we were both reasonably well known to the Germans, I decided not to make any attempt at exchanging identities until the actual day of departure from Schubin.

Since any change would have to be permanent, I decided that McDiarmid and I would also have to switch identity cards. This was complicated by the fact that the Germans checked identities by fingerprints as well as by photographs. Taking a chance, I joined one of the working parties of orderlies used to carry bread from the German compound across the road to the prison camp. On my second attempt, while in the German buildings, I was able to obtain three blank German identity cards. I found them lying on a desk where one of the German clerical staff had been checking through all the camp's cards.

Taking the cards back to our own compound, I obtained the use of a typewriter by breaking into the hospital office, and typed out particulars about McDiarmid and myself on each respective new card. I also transposed our fingerprints. However, in spite of four attempts, I was unable to get hold of our photographs from the genuine German identity cards.

As luck would have it, though, I got my chance to switch the photographs on the day that the final check of all the camp was made – but I also received a nasty shock. That day, a number of orderlies were detailed to help the Germans lay out our identity cards for checking. I dressed up as an orderly and presented myself with the other orderlies to help the Germans. In the confusion, I was able to obtain the original cards for both McDiarmid and myself.

It was then that I got the shock. I found that the genuine German identity cards had been partly typed and partly handwritten. In addition, certain notations had been made against the originals. The point was that these unexpected variations would prevent my substituting the cards I had so carefully prepared. Following the only possible course, I took the two genuine German cards up to my hut, where I got some glue and quickly transposed the two photos of McDiarmid and myself.

Dashing back, I managed to slip the cards back into their respective boxes without any of the Germans realizing that they been removed. The big snag was, though, that now I had to depend on the altered photographs alone getting me through the German check. The fingerprint check, I realized only too well, could lead to the Germans discovering the changed identities. However, in the event, the check at Schubin went through quite satisfactorily – and, to my great joy, I proceeded to leave Schubin PoW camp as Private John McDiarmid.

The date was now June 1943. When I arrived at Sagan, I managed to survive another identity check, but I had a close shave on my second day there. It turned out that at least four people besides myself had attempted an identity change. However, these people had not bothered to switch identity cards, too. Consequently, when a complete check was made of all the newly-arrived prisoners, four people who had done nothing other than exchange identities (but had not taken the precaution of also switching identity cards) were immediately caught by the Germans. They were promptly taken off to do the normal seven days' solitary confinement as punishment. Fortunately, I managed to come through this extra check undetected – obviously due to the fact that I had changed our photos. The incorrect fingerprints were, luckily, not discovered.

I took on normal orderly duties immediately I entered Sagan, much to the amusement of my aircrew friends. I made a point of getting to know the German guards well, so that my identity as an orderly should never be questioned. I also went out of my way to volunteer for any outside jobs going – for my idea at that stage was to try to escape from one of these working parties. However, as it turned out, we were always accompanied by German guards – never once did I get an opportunity to slip away.

Finally, in desperation, I decided to get myself sent to a troops' camp, from which escape would be much easier. The tactics I adopted were to volunteer for every job the Germans called for – and then, immediately I was placed on some unpleasant duty, to refuse to work. I would throw down my tools – and tell the Germans pointblank that I had no intention of carrying out their orders.

The reaction of the Huns to my stand, after three or four times, was quite definite. A German officer told me in no uncertain manner that the next time I adopted these tactics I would be sent away from Sagan. The point was that Sagan was considered to be a good camp for orderlies, whereas if I were to be transferred to Lamsdorf, as they threatened, I would be liable to be forced to work on farms, in coal mines or on any other less pleasant duties that the Germans chose. This, of course, was exactly what I wanted; and, after another couple of refusals, I was, in fact, sent to Lamsdorf. My chances of escape were now considerably improved.

When I was leaving Sagan, I learned of the German system of forcing privates to do whatever jobs cropped up – whereas NCOs could pick the type of work they preferred. Accordingly, when I entered Lamsdorf, I immediately promoted myself to corporal. My correct title, I told the Germans, was Corporal McDiarmid, not

Private. The security check was rather vague – and my entry as corporal was never questioned. Because of my new rank, I was now able to volunteer for a working party – and was immediately selected as a worker to go out to a farm just outside Breslay. Events were now playing into my hands.

After a few days on the farm, I saw that an escape attempt would be comparatively easy. Though we prisoners were supervised by a German guard, so few men had attempted to escape working parties that the average guard, after a couple of days, was quite prepared to accept the fact that his prisoners had no thoughts of escape. In addition, because prisoners were employed over a fairly dispersed area, and since no check was made between lunch-time and evening count, an escaping prisoner could get some distance before his absence was discovered.

After the lunch-hour break on my fourth day at the farm, I waited till the guard and the other prisoners had gone down to a paddock. Then I left the yard in which I was working – and struck out across country.

I decided that my best way to escape was to try to reach one of the Baltic ports. So I made directly for Danzig, with the object of obtaining a ship to Sweden. I took the precaution of carrying with me a pitchfork, which would signify to any passing German that I was a workman travelling to his job – and therefore not worth querying. Stealing a bicycle, I cycled along in daytime only, since the chance of being picked up was greater at night. On the fifth night, I entered Danzig.

My best bet, I thought, would be to locate a French working camp. My idea was to find someone there who would shelter me for the night and also help me to get aboard a Swedish ship. Eventually, I spotted a party of workmen who were obviously French. They were guarded by one German sentry who was taking little interest in his guard duties. I walked up to a Frenchman as unostentatiously as possible and finally managed to convince him that I was a British Air Force officer trying to escape. The Frenchman told me I could go back to his camp for the night, to hide from the Germans.

Borrowing my acquaintance's beret, and generally trying to look as much like a Frenchman as possible, I joined the party of Frenchmen. My friend told me that I should be able to enter the working party compound without difficulty, as the German guards rarely carried out checks. Sure enough, the whole party went straight into the camp – and the German guard did no more than chat to the sentry who accompanied us. Obviously, he worked on the principle that, while many people might try to escape, no one would be so foolish as to want to enter a prison camp. So I now found myself a guest of the Germans for the night!

Next day, the Camp Leader went out with a working party on duty on one of the wharves to try to arrange for me to get aboard a ship. Since I could not remain in the camp without fear of detection, I had to wander around the streets of Danzig all day. In the evening, I casually joined the returning party and got back into camp all right. To my joy, I then learned that the Camp Leader had contacted a Frenchman who would be working on a ship that was to leave for Sweden at seven o'clock the next night.

The following morning, I went with the working party to the wharves. I took the place of a Frenchman who had arranged to report sick; and, showing his papers, I got into the prohibited area without difficulty. About three o'clock in the afternoon, I discreetly made my way to the coal bunkers – in which I decided to stow away. I practically covered myself with coal, leaving only sufficient of the black lumps away from my head to ensure that I would be able to breathe easily.

About three hours later, following a sudden rush of activity, we sailed from the wharf and made our way out to open water. Up till this stage, I had noticed no definite search of the ship – and was beginning to congratulate myself on my good fortune in getting away undiscovered. However, my hopes were suddenly dashed. A little while after leaving the wharf, we anchored again and waited about half an hour. I soon began to realize that the reason for this stoppage was to enable customs or police officials to search the ship – and I now became uneasily aware that the search had actually begun.

Since I was fairly near the top of the coal, I could plainly hear any sounds of activity nearby. After a while, I was horrified to hear a German voice calling out in English that he knew an Englishman was concealed aboard – and that it was useless trying to hide. Worse, the German added that, unless the prisoner gave himself up immediately, he would suffer severe consequences when caught.

However, I assumed that this was probably a normal German safety precaution carried out on every search. So I remained where I was – hoping that my presence would not be discovered. But, once again, I was disappointed. To my dismay, I saw the covers removed from the bunker in which I was hiding. This fresh threat looked bad, for the Germans also had dogs on my track. A moment later, one Alsatian quickly intimated that he had scented something other than coal – me!

The Germans were now fairly certain that someone was, in fact, hiding on the ship. A moment later, a voice called out that, unless the person hiding in the bunkers gave himself up, the Germans would use tear-gas bombs – and so force him to come up. I still was not certain whether or not the Germans were bluffing. So I remained where I was.

However, true to their threats, the Germans did use tear-gas bombs; and, because I was so close to the top of the coal, and since I was in a very confined area, I found that it was not long before I was coughing and spluttering. My eyes began to stream, and I had involuntarily to give away my hiding place. Then I had to come up.

The Germans did not handle me particularly gently. When they got me to a type of barracks nearby, I admitted that I was a corporal in the Seaforth Highlanders who had escaped. The Huns were not over-impressed with my story, and checked up with my PoW camp at Lamsdorf. Fortunately, the check confirmed my story; and, since I could also substantiate my account by quoting my PoW identity number (actually McDiarmid's, of course), the Germans sent me back to Lamsdorf.

Before I left Danzig, I talked to one of the Germans who had helped to capture me. He told me that a Frenchman on the wharves had given me away. The Frenchman had seen me on the dock-side and had realized that I was not a fellow-countryman. Then, when he had noticed that I was no longer present, just before the ship had sailed, he had realized that I had gone on board. So he had told the Germans that he was certain an Englishman was trying to stow away. That was why the Germans had carried out a thorough search, and had caught me so easily.

However, when I was returned to Lamsdorf, the same thought continued to dominate my mind: I was still determined to escape.

Having considered the various possibilities. I finally decided that my best chance of escaping would be to try to go right across Germany, down through France, and with the help of the French *Maquis*, cross the Pyrenees into Spain. The big snag, however, was that languages were not my strong point. But I had a bit of luck in that I met a New Zealander, N. Geoffrey Williamson, who spoke excellent German and French, and who had himself already been out on a couple of escape attempts. Because my own escape would be seriously hampered by my lack of languages, it was agreed that Williamson and I should get out together. Our plan was to travel by train through Germany and into France, where we hoped to pick up a French Underground party who would help us to get back to England. We worked out all details carefully in advance, being given considerable help by two Canadians, Sergeant Larry Pals and Sergeant Major McLean.

*

On Sunday, 19 September 1943, following our carefully-arranged plan, we secretly changed into our workman's clothes – and lowered ourselves into the tunnel through which we planned to escape. We were equipped with forged identity papers to establish our 'bona fides' as French volunteer workmen returning from a munitions factory at Blechhammer. I also carried a letter from the Blechhammer camp doctor stating that I was suffering from a type of laryngitis which prevented me from speaking in anything above a hoarse whisper. This precaution was, of course, to ensure that my lack of languages should not be detected.

Our plan necessitated getting out of the tunnel in broad daylight. This was tricky, because German sentries were stationed every fifty yards along the wire. To ensure that the attention of the German guards was distracted, McLean and Pals arranged for a camp game of baseball to take place immediately in front of the sentrybox nearest the mouth of the tunnel. In addition, they organized a football match near the next box along the wire – with some lively scrummages going on to rivet the German's attention on the game. Our main danger was the sentry-box immediately in front of the point from which we were to break out of the tunnel. A fairly intricate system of signalling was accordingly set up to give us the word when to attempt the break. The danger was complicated by the fact that odd German civilians, some of whom wandered into the camp vicinity on Sunday afternoons, might see us.

Williamson and I waited anxiously underneath the trap at the end of the tunnel. It was not until some quarter of an hour had passed – which seemed to us like eternity – that, at long last, we received the signal to break. To make certain that the German guard remained completely oblivious of the breathtaking events going on twenty yards behind his back, the baseball game suddenly developed into a bout of fist-icuffs between two of the players. The fighting had developed into a violent scrap by the time Williamson and myself finally, after a lot of exertion, managed to push the wooden trap off the tunnel. Then we levered the trap up sufficiently to enable Williamson to crawl out. Immediately, he went into some scrub bushes some thirty yards from the camp fence.

I came out right behind him. Then I lay flat on my stomach while I gradually dropped the trap back into place. Afterwards I scraped dirt and grass over the top. I patted this camouflage in as quickly as I could – so that the tunnel location would remain reasonably concealed, ready for use again at a later date.

This was probably the most nerve-racking part of the escape. At any moment, a German might unexpect-edly come along. Worse, a guard might suddenly tire of watching the game, casually look round – and see me lying on the ground in rather an awkward position, obviously attempting to escape. The snag was that the German guard would stand little chance of stopping me with a bayonet. So his immediate reaction would be to shoot. Consequently, being stuck out there in broad daylight was, to say the least, a little unnerving.

Fortunately, however, everything went according to plan – and I joined Williamson without an alarm being raised. Then we strolled slowly down the side of the camp wires. To make our presence appear quite normal, we even stopped for a few seconds to watch the fight that was still going on in the baseball match. We did not move on, in fact, until a guard told us that civilians were not allowed to loiter near the camp!

We then wandered nonchalantly on as if we were out for an afternoon stroll. Sauntering down through the German barrack quarters, we went past the main gate of the camp and on to the road leading to Lamsdorf Station. Our plan was to catch a train to Breslay, where we would pick up the Berlin Express. We hoped to reach Berlin by ten o'clock that night.

At the station, Williamson bought two tickets without difficulty. Then we boarded the train, which pulled in some ten minutes after we arrived. We stood in the midst of a large number of German soldiers on the rear platform of one of the carriages – and our presence aroused absolutely no comment. At Breslay, Williamson again simply walked up to the booking-office window, asked for two tickets to Berlin – and obtained them without query.

On the way to Berlin, however, I received a nasty jolt when we passed through Sagan, the PoW camp which I had left only a few weeks previously. Somewhat to my consternation, waiting on Sagan station to join the Express, were three guards whom I had known quite well in Sagan prison camp. What was worse, because of my orderly duties, they knew me equally well. Fortunately, I was standing in a carriage which was very full; and, as it turned out, the guards got aboard several carriages farther down the train.

This encounter put me on my guard for the rest of the journey – for it made me realize that there was a chance of my being recognized when I left the train at Berlin. So I asked Williamson also to keep a sharp look-out for the German guards. Luckily, however, by the time we reached Berlin it was dark. What with the effective black-out restrictions, and the colossal congestion on the station, we were easily swallowed up in the crowd. We walked out of the station with a sigh of relief.

Our problem now was to find accommodation for the night. However, we felt quite confident that our papers and appearance would get us by. So we went across to a hotel opposite the station, where we obtained accommodation without difficulty. When we had left camp, we had been warned that all hotel lists were checked by German officials each morning – and that anyone unusual was often interrogated. To safeguard ourselves against the risk of unwittingly falling into the Germans' hands again, we therefore arranged for coffee and bread and jam to be served in our room at 7 am. The pretext we gave was that we had an early train to catch. Next morning, we left our hotel at about 7.30 am, travelled across Berlin by underground, then caught a train to Mannheim, on our way to Sarrbrucken.

When we arrived at Mannheim at about 10 pm, we

were unable to obtain accommodation for the night because of damage inflicted on the city by RAF bombing. So we spent the night in an air-raid shelter under the railway station. This turned out to be a particularly nasty experience – since, for some twenty minutes, we found ourselves on the receiving end of an RAF raid.

Next morning, while waiting for our train, we had a haircut and shave, and travelled round the city by tram. This was to avoid the risk of being questioned by the police, who seemed to be keeping a pretty strict check on people moving in and out of the city. We were fortunate in making this decision, I learned later, for the Germans had a tight cordon thrown round the city to prevent people working under forced labour in Germany from escaping under cover of the confusion caused by the bombing. Later, we caught our train to Saarbrucken.

Following our pre-arranged plan, when we reached Saarbrucken, we made contact with a man called Pierre. He was employed on a French working party – and was in contact with smuggling gangs who operated between the French and German areas. His contacts would get us across the frontier, under cover of darkness, without running any real risk of capture.

One of the younger Frenchmen at the working-party camp once got us into what could have been quite a sticky spot. The trouble was that the Frenchman seemed to get a real kick out of insulting Germans to their faces. On this occasion, Williamson and I were having coffee and biscuits at a local cafe. Suddenly, I was dismayed to see two French lads walk up to some Germans and blatantly tell them, with obvious relish, that they could hoodwink them. To my horror, they went on to say that they could probably help people to escape right under the Huns' noses! Naturally, Williamson and I beat a hasty retreat.

Next, we proceeded to Metz, which was right on the scene of smuggling operations. Meanwhile, we had picked up a companion – Georges Monclard. He was a Frenchman who wanted to escape from German forced labour to return to his home in Marseilles. We decided to cross into France together. Later, we met the guide who was to take us across the border. He was an eighteen-year-old Frenchman who went over the border two or three times a week to visit his family and girl-friend.

On the night on which we decided to cross the frontier, we caught a train up to the station immediately before the border. Then we set out to walk along the main road towards the frontier itself. Following the road to within about three-quarters of a mile of the patrol point, we cut across paddocks at right angles to the border until we came to a point where our guide maintained that the crossing could easily be made.

At this point, the border was patrolled by a German

guard who covered an area of about one mile along the wire. Each guard was equipped with a rifle, and, in certain cases, an Alsatian dog. In addition, normal searchlight posts were situated along the wire at about one-mile intervals. The border, I now discovered, consisted of two barbed-wire fences. These were about four feet high and about fifty yards apart. We decided to go across individually. Our guide went first – taking with him his ten-year-old brother, who was returning home. Then came Williamson, followed by Georges. I brought up the rear.

Everything went according to plan until Williamson slipped as he attempted to get through the far wire. Since the wires were fairly loose, Williamson's sudden movement caused a certain amount of noise. The slight sound, carried through the still air, immediately attracted the attention of the German sentry some distance away. Though the night was fairly dark, the sentry could obviously see that something was happening in the wire. Immediately, he rushed up to Williamson, who was still inside the wire – and held him up at rifle point. What was I to do?

*

The German sentry pointed his rifle menacingly at Williamson. The Hun had my friend completely at his mercy – for he had just caught him red-handed, in the middle of the night, trying to cross the frontier.

However, for some unknown reason, the sentry did not raise an alarm to attract the other guards. Nor, fortunately, in the darkness, did he see either Georges or myself. At once, jabbing his rifle threateningly towards my fellow-escaper, he began to question Williamson in German as to what he was doing in the forbidden zone.

We were obviously in a pretty tough spot; for, I realized, no matter how good a story Williamson told, he was now quite certain to be arrested. Taking all the factors into consideration, I made up my mind to liquidate the guard. Fortunately, the Hun was so excited as he interrogated Williamson that he was totally unaware of my presence as I crawled silently up behind him. I moved so quietly, in fact, that even Williamson did not know I was in the vicinity.

Suddenly, I made a wild leap at the guard: I got a good hold around his throat. My fingers closed around his windpipe before he had a chance to yell out. My object was to choke him into insensibility to prevent his raising the alarm.

When Williamson and the others saw what was happening, they all rushed to my assistance. Georges took the rifle from the German, who had, in any case, dropped it when I had attacked him. Because of the stranglehold I had on him, the guard was still unable to utter a word.

In the circumstances, I had no alternative but to go on increasing the pressure until I felt the guard lose consciousness. As soon as I was absolutely certain that he was unconscious, I dropped him to the ground. Then we picked up our packs, clambered through the wire – and raced off at top speed. Shortly afterwards we reached the small village of Aubouie, where we hid in a loft.

However, we now wanted to get out of this area as quickly as possible: for if the Germans should link us with the incident of the unconscious sentry, the consequences for us would not be pleasant. Our task now was to leave the area before the Germans organized a search. Fortunately, a few hours later, Georges Monclard found out that we could get a bus out of the village. Accordingly at about six o'clock in the morning we dashed down to the village square – and climbed aboard a bus.

The trouble, however, was that Georges tended to be a little bit irrational on some occasions. In this instance, to our dismay, we found that the bus on which we were travelling was taking us back across the border into German territory! It operated non-stop to Briey, a minor tail junction straddled right across the new border line. Since we could not leave the bus without arousing suspicion, we just had to stay where we were until the vehicle took us back into the German area. The abuse that I hurled at Georges when we finally left the bus was sufficient to stop many a man in his tracks.

However, Georges made up for his sins later on by

getting us back across into French territory. He made contact with the driver of a train about to leave for Luneville – and the driver kindly arranged to get us through. Leading the way down to the marshalling yards, Georges went up to an engine that was taking on water. Sure enough, George's engine-driver friend invited us up into the cab. Then he covered us with a couple of old great-coats and some sacks, so that we would not be seen by the German guards.

When his engine had taken on water, he shunted up on a track immediately alongside the carriages he was waiting to pick up. Then, leaning out, he opened the door of a second-class compartment. When the driver got the 'all-clear' from a guard on the platform the three of us jumped across into the compartment. A couple of minutes later, we were handed our tickets by the guard.

On our journey to Luneville we again encountered the desire of certain Frenchmen to share their secrets with everyone. As our train rattled along. Georges calmly informed a French farmer and his wife sharing our compartment that Williamson and I were Allied soldiers on the last part of our escape from Germany to England. When the French couple got out after a comparatively short journey, I began to fear that possibly they might give us away to the German authorities. However, evidently they did not do so, for we eventually arrived in Luneville quite safely.

Through Georges, we now made contact with a leading citizen in Luneville, in whose house we stayed. While there, we were introduced to the chief *gendarme*. This official told us that he hoped to arrange for us to be taken down to the Spanish border. The Chief of Police also issued us with authentic French identity cards and put all our other papers in order.

Later, on his orders, we were taken to Nancy. We were handcuffed and escorted on the journey by two *gendarmes*, since, ostensibly, we were being taken there to be imprisoned for stealing. The ruse worked excellently. Then, when we arrived in Nancy, we had our photographs taken – and these pictures were affixed to our identity cards, so that our papers were now a hundred per cent genuine.

By devious means, arranged by the French Underground, we subsequently went on to Ruffec, in the Franco-Spanish border region. In Ruffec, we met the Comtesse de Melville, who was known as 'Marie'. She was an Englishwoman who was running an escape organization. She told us that the best way home was to cross the Pyrenees into Spain, then to go to a British Consulate or else press on to Gibraltar. The Chief of Police in Ruffec also saw that our papers were all right, so we were now all set to cross into Spain.

While we waited at Ruffec, Williamson and I were joined by two Polish escapers, both RAF sergeants. The four of us were to cross the Pyrenees from Foix, not far from the border. A hitch developed on our first trip to Foix, so we returned to Ruffec.

To my dismay, when a new route was fixed up shortly afterwards, I had to stay behind. The reason was that a danger of interrogation existed on this new route – and I was the only member of the party who could not speak fluent French. When I saw Williamson and the two Poles set off without me, I felt a lot of regret and a certain amount of envy since they were taking the first opportunity of making the final escape. I didn't realize at the time that this change in plan probably helped to save my life; for, within thirty-six hours, Williamson was to lose his life in a Pyrenees blizzard that developed during his crossing.

Two days after Williamson's departure, I was joined at Ruffec by four more escapers. They were Captain R. B. ('Buck') Palm, of the South African Air Force; an RAF Flying Officer, Michael Cooper, who came from Kenya; and two Canadians from the same crew, Flying Officer Harry Smith, a navigator, and Sergeant Len Martin, a wireless operator. These were the men with whom I was to make my desperate attempt to escape.

*

A few days after their arrival, an unexpected complication arose. We suddenly found ourselves in the midst of a violent quarrel for the leadership of our escape organization. The quarrel arose when a French woman who had helped us to escape from Nancy, and whom I believe was a Countess, arrived in Ruffec. She immediately began to assert to Marie that only she was capable of getting us back to England. It soon became evident that the struggle for power was going to be most bitter. Weighing up the pros and cons, we settled the issue by unanimously deciding to stay with Marie.

After another hitch, we eventually set out to cross the Pyrenees. We began our journey in a truck. But, as we were going round a mountain road, we suddenly heard a loud crack at the back – and quickly came to rest on the roadside with a broken back axle. However, we eventually reached Tardets, from which we were to start out on foot on our tough trek across the mountains.

Our idea, of course, was to reach Spain. But I had already heard many stories of escapers who had been given rough treatment in Spanish prison camps. So I took an important precaution: I carried with me letters addressed to the British Consuls at San Sebastian and Barcelona and to the British Ambassador at Madrid. These letters advised the British authorities that we had crossed the frontier and would be in a certain area. The envelopes were already addressed in Spanish and franked with Spanish stamps. So, after adding in the name of the place in which we were likely to be imprisoned, all I had to do was to post them. These letters, I was fairly sure, would probably help to hasten our rescue by the British authorities.

About one o'clock in the morning, we set out by moonlight on the last phase of our journey. Two Basque guides led us. After about an hour's walking, rain started to fall. Later, this developed into a steady drizzle, which saturated us all. Harry Smith felt the strain of our tough trek fairly badly: and, by about four o'clock in the morning, he had reached the stage where he found it virtually impossible to go any farther without rest.

We now had to cross a main road actively patrolled by Germans. We also had to go over a bridge which was normally guarded by German sentries. Because of Harry's illness, we left him in an old cattle barn for a few minutes while we reconnoitred the immediate area to find out the best way of avoiding the patrols. However, when we came to the bridge, we saw a dark shape standing by the side. Fearing the worst, we assumed that the Germans kept the bridge guarded all the time.

Crossing the mountain stream without using the bridge involved a long detour, which would disrupt the guides' plans. So we decided to wait until daybreak to find out definitely what chance we had of getting over the bridge. When morning came, we were much relieved to find that what we had thought was a German guard was, in fact, nothing more than an old post leaning up against the side of the railings with a bag flapping from its top. In the darkness, this post had looked from the distance like someone standing with a rifle slung over his shoulder.

By the time we had had a meal at an inn on the other side of the bridge, Harry had improved so much that he felt capable of carrying on for the rest of the trip. However, as we trudged up a steep slope on the next part of the route, the incessant drizzle got worse. First, it changed to sleet, then it became a solid snow storm. Shortly afterwards, the snow storm gradually assumed the proportions of a blizzard. The wind blew great gusts of snow all over us. Our shoes and clothes became sopping wet. Then, as the snow got deeper, walking became more difficult. Eventually conditions got so bad that it became almost impossible to maintain any decent foothold.

On one occasion, we had to cross a razor-like ridge connecting two peaks. The width of the track was not more than about two feet six inches – with a sheer drop of 200 to 300 feet on either side. Because of the wind which was constantly plucking at us, and since it was almost impossible to retain a firm foot-hold, we had to cross this ridge practically on hands and knees. Desperately we hoped that nothing unexpected would happen – for even a small slip would send us hurtling over the edge to instant death. The crossing seemed to take ages. However, we eventually accomplished it safely.

By evening we found a type of mountain shack. We decided to spend the night there, in an attempt to regain some warmth and strength. However, the cold was so bitter that we could not get any decent rest. So, after a few hours, we were forced to push on again. It soon became obvious that our guides were completely lost. All we could do was to keep heading southwest, so that at least we were making slow progress in the right direction.

Half-way through the day, our guides wanted to turn back. They had had enough, they said. However, we were determined to carry on – and told the guides so in no uncertain fashion. But both guides were feeling the strain badly. Their exertions were telling on them so much, that, as we progressed, they became extremely vehement in their desire to turn back. But the guides had been paid something like 15,000 francs each to take us across; and, since, in any case, we could not make our way back with any degree of certainty, we were more or less forced to insist that they carry on.

Now Mike Cooper began to crack up. He was so weary, he said, that he was just going to sit down and rest. On one occasion, I found Mike missing. Retracing our steps, Buck Palm and myself discovered him a quarter of a mile back, lying in the snow in a low state. Obviously, if he had lain there any length of time, he would gradually have lost consciousness and would have died in the blizzard. Between the two of us, we managed to get Mike back on his feet. Then we pummelled him back into some sense of consciousness – and he forced himself to keep going.

Now, once more, Harry Smith did not feel terribly fit. And, of course, we also had to help Mike. To add to our difficulties, the elder guide soon showed signs of cracking up. His feet were so badly frost-bitten that he could barely walk. To make matters worse, we were all so tired that we found difficulty in continuing to help our guide and Mike.

The guide was in such a bad state that he eventually found it impossible to continue any longer. We massaged his hands and feet in an endeavour to restore his circulation. But, in a very short time, he completely lost consciousness. Now we had a difficult decision to make. If we all remained with the guide, in the open, with the blizzard still raging, the rest of us would succumb in a matter of an hour or so. However, if we left the guide where he was, he would certainly never regain consciousness, and would die. Taking into account all the factors, we eventually decided that to press on, leaving the guide behind, was the only possible course we could adopt.

While we were trying to make the guide comfortable, we were astonished to see another traveller coming towards us. He turned out to be a Spaniard – and he kindly gave us all a drink of light wine he was carrying in a skin water bag. He also tried to force some of the wine down the throat of our Basque guide. Five minutes later, the Spaniard continued on his way.

We could still do nothing for our guide. So, covering him with a groundsheet, and making him as comfortable as possible, we left him where he was. Then we straggled off on our bitter journey.

After going about a mile, I was dismayed to see that Mike Cooper had entirely disappeared again. Rather than leave him to the same fate as our guide, I went back – and found him lying in the snow about a quarter of a mile behind us. He was so close to unconsciousness that he could not speak. I doubt if he even recognized me when I shook him. Then Len Martin came back to tell me that a small hut had been spotted by the rest of our party. It was, he said, down by a creek bank, about a mile and a half farther on.

My idea now was to get the guide and Mike down to the shelter of the hut right away. Leaving Mike for a few minutes, I went back to the guide. I found him practically covered in snow – and obviously dead.

I got back to Mike as quickly as possible, and was able to half-drag and half-carry him down the hill on to the banks of the creek. The others helped me to take him the rest of the way.

We forced an entry into the hut, lit a fire to dry out our clothes and got some much-needed rest.

We set off again at about nine o'clock next morning. Our remaining guide led us down a river, which we hoped would eventually bring us out to some Spanish village. To my amazement, when we came to a junction of two streams, our guide insisted that we follow the other stream. We argued with him over this decision. But our guide maintained that he could quickly lead us to a village.

However, after following him for about five or ten minutes, we decided his directions were wrong. So, checking our bearings with the compass, we turned back and followed the original stream. Eventually we came out on a main road, which led us to a type of frontier outpost manned by Spanish police. Since we were all in such a bad state, we handed ourselves over to the Spaniards, who, after giving us a meal, accompanied us to the nearest village.

We were taken to the local police station. But, before we got there, I found out where letters could be posted. On the way, I dropped my letters addressed to various British representatives into the box. Later, we were collected by a British representative from the Embassy in Madrid; and safe again in British care, we were eventually taken to Gibraltar, from where we were flown back to England.

When our Dakota came in to land at its English airfield, a strong crosswind was blowing. The pilot it seemed to me, was not making a particularly good job of his landing. My judgement was, in fact, borne out a moment later. Immediately after touching down, our aircraft swung right-off the runway, skidded across the grass and bowled over a parked Anson. Eventually, the

Dak came to a rather ignominious stop – with one wing badly damaged and the undercarriage messed up. All of us eighteen passengers heaved a sigh of relief at having got down safely.

However, though I had made a somewhat shaky arrival, my escape was now, thank goodness, all over. I was a free man at last.

*

After his return to England, Allan McSweyn served in Transport Command for the remainder of the war. His daring escape brought him the award of the Military Cross. Demobilized in 1946, he subsequently became Queensland Manager of Trans-Australian Airlines, Brisbane.

Brigadier James Hargest was born in New Zealand in 1891, after distinguished service in Egypt, Galipoli and France during the First World War he spent fourteen years as a member of the New Zealand Parliament. In January 1940 he left New Zealand as commander of the Fifth Infantry Brigade, going first to England and then to the Middle East. His brigade defended the Olympus Pass in Greece in 1941, and afterwards he led 4,000 troops in the defence of Maleme airfield in Crete. Only 900 returned to Egypt.

In November 1941 Hargest was captured at Sidi Aziz during the Second Libyan Campaign and imprisoned in Compo No 12 *near Florence, the PoW camp reserved for high-ranking British officers. It was from there that he made his escape, as this story relates.*

4

Farewell *Campo 12*

On Sunday, 28 March, it rained hard. As the day advanced we made ready. There was, of course, a certain amount of tension and when at church service we found that G-P had included the hymn 'Through the night of doubt and sorrow onwards goes the pilgrim band', we were all a little moved. Right up till seven-thirty we thought there were great possibilities; but with night the rain eased and Neame cancelled preparations; needless to say there were divergent opinions, but we had agreed to abide by his decision, and there was never any question of the wisdom of this.

Monday morning was fine; but as the day advanced clouds came over and by six o'clock it was raining hard, a silent rain, but very close to what we needed. I was on my bed resting at about 7.30 pm when Neame looked in and said: 'I think you had better dress, Jim; it looks as though tonight will be a good one.'

At once we got to work and in a very few minutes I was ready. Ranfurly had reserved some sandwiches and hard-boiled eggs for each of us, and at the last I opened a bottle of rum which Stirling and I had kept for this occasion for over a year. I filled six two- or three-ounce medicine bottles, one for each man. There was also room for a small bottle of wine in my case.

Then came the hardest moment of the whole adventure; saying good-bye to Howes. For three years we had been together, in England and in the East. We had fought together; on all my leaves however short, I had taken him. In the Greek and Cretan campaigns he had never left me for one moment, no matter how weary he was, and in our last fight he had shared my slit trench. He was a big, quiet young fellow who inspired confidence; in Vincigliate every officer and man liked and respected him. Of course, he wanted to come with me, I would have given much to take him, but the risks were great and the chances of success so small that I did not feel I had a right to endanger him. So we said good-bye. War is hard in its good-byes.

Dinner was a quarter of an hour earlier that night and we sat down all together for the last time, some of the boys mounting guard to prevent surprise. While we were dining Neame and Ranfurly passed through the hole into the chapel, Neame to see that all was right in the tunnel, Ranfurly to pull down the timbering at the far end and cut away the remaining earth up to the surface. He took the long knife and made a perfect job.

We were all waiting rather tensely, trying to conceal it beneath the veneer of small talk, when the last alarm came through from Vaughan's room: 'Officer coming.' We six escapees took up our cases and fled upstairs through the living-rooms. It was only an NCO making his round of the battlements. We trooped back to the dining-room. Things ran smoothly from then onwards. We said our good-byes lightheartedly and one by one filed into the lift-landing and slid for the last time through the panel into the chapel porch. I was fourth man and when I got in the first three had disappeared down the shaft. Ranfurly was sitting, naked except for a pair of shorts, at the head of the shaft, and when I went to shake hands he said: 'For heaven's sake don't touch me, I'm just one greasy slimy mess from head to foot.' Taking out those last five inches of mud had been a dirty business.

I found Neame sitting in the by-pass. He reported that all was well. He had shaded light there, and I could see Boyd's legs disappearing up the ladder. Each of us had a special task once we appeared on the surface. John Combe went first carrying his suitcase, a stout rope and a blanket. The blanket he spread on the ground to act as a carpet to avoid obvious marks a sentry could see when daylight came. The rope was to be hitched round a post on the top of a stone wall just down the hillside from the battlements. It was our last obstacle, five feet high on the uphill side and about ten feet on the downhill or road side. The rope was to steady us; we could hang on to it while descending. A huge iron gate about twelve feet high opened on to the road. As we had never seen it used in all the time we had been there we had no reason to hope that it might not be locked. Once over, John was to help Miles, who was then to be his assistant on the road. Miles, second man up, was to take a measured three-ply board reinforced for strengthening, to be used as a lid for the hole when the last man was out. Boyd was next and had just his kit. He was to get on to the road and act as scout while the rest came over.

I was number four and in addition to my suitcase had the hooked rope we always used for haulage and a sandbag full of pine needles and soil. I pushed the case up ahead of me, and dragged the sandbag up with my free hand – not easy in that confined space with mud oozing out from every side. When I emerged I had a shock. Instead of the darkness we had expected a couple of concealed lamps made it almost as light as day. Had an Italian been on that side he must have seen each of us as we came up. As it happened, the light certainly made our exit easy.

It was a tremendous experience. Not even the need for action could suppress the wave of exaltation that swept over me. Here was the successful achievement of a year of planning and seven months of toil. I remember thinking, with a new kind of awareness, that whatever the immediate future held, at this moment I was alive and free. I have never been able to recapture in retrospect the fullness of that moment.

I put down my case and sandbag and passed the rope back into the shaft, hook downwards. A tug, and I began hauling up. Carton's large pack appeared. I unhooked it and fished again, this time for O'Connor's pack. All this was according to plan and I had hauled in and was waiting for a head and shoulders to appear when a whisper came up: 'The rope.' A bit surprised, I tried again; up came two walking sticks – I hadn't heard about them. De Wiart came surprisingly easily. As he surfaced I placed his pack on the stump of his left arm and off he went. O'Connor, following, disappeared into the darkness. I threw the carpet back down the shaft and clamped the board over the hole. It fitted perfectly and stood my weight as I pressed it down. I emptied my bag of pine needles on it and smoothed the surface. I even found a few stones and some chickweed to give it a natural appearance. The last job was to level off any remaining footmarks. Then, taking up my case, rope and empty sack, I decamped. It was exactly half-past nine.

They were all waiting at the foot of the little wall. We had had unexpected good luck, as the door to the road was not locked, and we passed through. I gave my rope to Miles, who cached it along with the other one in a place already chosen, not too conspicuous, yet not too well hidden. When our flight was discovered we hoped that they would be found and give the impression that we had come over the top. We wanted to keep the secret of the tunnel as long as possible. Once through the door we found sufficient shadows to make the going safer. We began crossing the road. John, finding the door difficult to close, slammed it; the noise seemed to shatter our freedom.

We filed down through the wet woods in complete darkness, then across a fence into an olive grove. Thick brambles made the terraces difficult to negotiate; but we got down somehow without noise. Half-way down to the deep valley we were making for we stopped and hid our overclothes and my sandbag in some bushes. Six hundred yards lower down a roadway ran at right angles to our path. Here we said good-bye to O'Connor and de Wiart, who were using this as a starting-point for their long walk. We shook hands, and the darkness swallowed them up.

The rain had stopped, and we had no trouble in seeing our way downhill to a bridge above a mill, where we came on a tarred road. We threw our overshoes into the swollen stream. I felt terribly dirty, and seemed to be mud all over, so I soused my suitcase in the running water and cleaned off the worst of it. Then we set off on our six-mile tramp. The road offered no obstacles, we knew it so well from observation, and we tramped along it like a police squad in pairs, our heavy boots making a tremendous noise. It was the first time in many months we had walked on a road unaccompanied by a guard, although I don't think we gave much thought to that at the time.

Once we got on to the lower ground nearer the city we began to meet people carrying torches or on lighted bicycles. We were a little tense at first; but no one took any notice of us and we soon became accustomed to them. We were dressed in very heavy clothes because we felt certain that if we succeeded in reaching the mountains near the frontier we would find snow and might have to sleep out in it. In addition, we wore our greatcoats and before long we felt the heat and perspired like oxen. For some reason Miles and Boyd, who were leading, cracked on a very fast pace that seemed unnecessary and even dangerous. I caught them up and suggested slowing down as we had three hours from the start in which to do six miles, and it would be preferable not to arrive too early and too hot. They were afraid that we might miss our route and wanted some time in hand. As it was, we arrived at 11.35 pm. After a little careful reconnaissance, we went boldly into the huge hall of the station.

The ticket gate was at the far end, guarded by *cara-binieri* and railway officials. We did not stay together but moved about separately to get the lie of the land. I wanted to see whether I drew any special attention, so took a position close to some soldiers in the middle of the great hall; but neither they nor anyone else looked at me or my dirty boots, so I gained fresh confidence and ceased to be afraid of being detected through my dress.

We drifted outside and met in the shadow, Boyd going off to buy three third-class return tickets to Milan. In a few moments he returned rather perturbed. In response to his request the ticket clerk had asked a question or told him something, and Boyd had fled. We thought it could be nothing more serious than instructions about changing at Bologna, so Miles went over and bought tickets without further trouble. Combe who was better dressed travelled second-class and bought his own ticket. The waiting was trying. To relieve the monotony we walked about the streets in pairs, coming back at intervals through the gates. It was quite simple. Adopting the slowish gait of an elderly workman I walked up and, looking each official in the eye as I reached him, passed safely through.

Then began a long wait. The train did not come in until 1.45 am. It was to have left at 12.35 am. Contrary to report, Fascism could not even run the trains punctually for us. All that time we walked about the cold, wet platform, afraid to sit down in case we sat on something forbidden – there were no regular seats.

When the train arrived it was crowded to the doors, and the chances of getting aboard seemed remote. The seething crowd on the platforms surged towards the doors in solid masses, preventing anyone from alighting. I saw a new technique in trainboarding. Men and women ranged themselves along the platform opposite the compartment windows; a man would heave his lady up until she got a hand-hold which enabled her to go through the window. Then she reached down and hauled in the baggage which the man held up to her, afterwards taking his arms and pulling him up and in. We were well separated by this time and I had no one to haul me in. I determined that if anyone was left behind it wasn't going to be me, and tucking my bag safely under my arm, I charged in. I don't know how I managed it, but eventually I got one foot on the step and the crowd behind did the rest, depositing me well into the corridor with Boyd not far behind. All this was done to the accompaniment of shouts, curses, and fierce arguments, in none of which I took part; but I was on board. I did not ask for more.

The Italians are wonderful people. At one moment they can hurl piercing diatribes at each other; at the next they are smiling and all politeness. In five minutes they were laughing and teasing and making room for each other like happy children. My only discomfort was due to the fact that the man next to me, not six inches from my face, was the *carabiniere* in charge of the carriage. After a while he began to talk to me. I ignored him, but he spoke again. I bent over and said in a whisper such as I've heard deaf people often use: 'I'm sorry, but I am very deaf.' This was in Italian and probably very bad Italian, though I had practised hard; but it was effective and he left me alone.

The train was fast and we did the forty-five miles to Bologna in an hour, arriving at 3 am. The slow train to Milan was due to leave precisely at that time, but actually it was twenty minutes past five before we got away. Another weary wait on a cold platform without any seats. Our efforts to find a refreshment buffet were fruitless. Once when the others were seeking food and I was watching the luggage, a policeman asked me if all the bags were mine. I said they were and he walked off. Several people asked me about platforms or trains, but my chief anxiety was the delay. It was growing lighter and our features would become easier to distinguish. We had hoped to be in Milan by six o'clock and at Como by eight; we seemed to be stuck here indefinitely.

When the train did come in the scrimmage was fiercer than at Florence. By this time, I had learnt from experience and, putting my head down, drove in, using my elbows on all who came alongside. By this method I got on to the step and mounted to the top; but then disaster overtook me. Someone clutched at my poor little suitcase and tore it out of my hand, leaving me only the handle. I had to make a quick decision – to retrieve it or leave it. I decided on the former, and kicking my legs clear I dropped straight down on the crowd struggling to mount the high steps. The cursing reached a high standard; but I found my bag and butting ahead with it climbed up again. This time I was farther along the corridor. I could see Miles' tall figure at the other end and Boyd about six feet behind me. We ignored each other.

I repaired the handle of my bag with a boot-lace, and standing with my back to the outside wall, held it behind my neck so that it would not be trampled on. My legs straddled a pile of suitcases on the floor. As soon as we started a little elderly man nearby spoke to me and threatened to become chatty. I looked straight at him with what I thought was a little smile, but was probably more like a foolish grin to him, and said nothing. When he persisted I repeated my formula about being deaf.

He turned away to find another audience, whom he amused by making jokes at my expense, all of which, of course, I had to ignore. He was a mean little man and I would have loved to wring his neck. The train stopped at every station and the journey seemed endless. I had memorized all the larger stations so that in the event of a hasty detrainment I would know where we were in relation to other places and to the frontier. I ticked them off as we passed: Modena, Parma, Piacenza,

Lodi – they came and went horribly slowly. From the beginning I had prayed that if we had to run for it we would at least be over the river Po; at last we crossed it. The heavy rain beat drearily across the Lombardy Plain. Every stream was in spate, in every hollow lakes had formed; the Po itself was wide and muddy.

In the corridor there was an air of jollity and no one seemed to resent the over-crowding; on the contrary, they enjoyed it. Near the door was a ladies' toilet and as we progressed the women in the carriage kept coming down to it, squeezing past everyone with great difficulty. One cheery old fellow installed himself as doorkeeper and as one woman came out he would call: 'One more!' If a lady overstayed a period he thought reasonable he would knock on the door and urge her to hurry. Everyone enjoyed him. As each woman passed me at my corner I had to crouch to make room and this brought my weight down on the cases below me. After a while I saw my troublesome old man look down intently. He struck a match to see better and held it near my feet. I looked down and a dreadful sight met my gaze. My weight had split the two or three cheap cases from top to bottom and out of the cracks appeared ladies' lingerie, gloves etc.; worst of all, there was a sickly red mess on the floor that was either red wine mixed with mud or strawberry jam – the match went out before I could decide. My position would have been bad if the old man or anyone nearby had been the owner and involved me in an argument of which the results could only have been disastrous. I prayed hard. The old man looked at me and winked. Obviously the bags weren't his. I determined to be well out of the carriage by the time the real owner could get to them.

At Lodi, the last stop before Milan, a nice-looking young woman and her husband got in. I don't quite know how they did it. Anyway, she was full of personality and in a very few moments she was the centre of much chattering. She seemed to be re-telling some joke the old man was making at the expense of Lodi, and tried to draw me into the talk. I smiled back weakly, and the old man came to my assistance: 'It's no use talking to him. He's deaf. Anyway, I think he's a German.'

*

We reached Milan at 8.20 am, the exact time a train was scheduled to leave for Como. The remarkable thing was that it left punctually. By the time we had all met and got our bearings on that huge station several minutes had elapsed, so we had to form another plan, a very difficult thing to do when we dared not stand together for any length of time. We threw suggestions as we passed and re-passed, and each of them seemed to be opposed to all the others.

I wanted to take a taxi as far along the Como road as we could, but that was rejected. Miles refused to believe the timetable which said that the next train ran at a little after midday, and went and bought four tickets for Como; but when we arrived at the ticket-gate we were told to come back at twelve o'clock, so we strode off and I chewed up my ticket as I went. I couldn't think of any other way to get rid of it. We took a stroll around a square and met for another discussion. John urged that we try the North Station, the terminus of a private line to Como situated some distance away. The majority agreed and Boyd and Combe set off. We saw them run for a tram and, as far as we could see, they caught it. We never saw them again. We waited for a few minutes and boarded another from different ends. There was a little lady near to me who appeared friendly so I asked her if she would tell me when to get off. She herself was going to the North Station; so I edged along and whispered to Miles to watch when she got off. I had always wanted to see Milan, especially the Scala Theatre and the Cathedral. That morning, I saw them both; we passed the Scala, and caught a view of the Cathedral as we crossed a piazza.

It was five minutes to ten when we arrived, and we saw that a train was scheduled to leave at ten-thirty for Como. No sign of the other two; we thought they might have bought their tickets already and gone through the gate. While Reg bought ours I went into the buffet and ordered coffee and newspapers, securing a window table from which we would be able to see the platform and any sign of the others. Reg was horrified when I opened my case and took out a sandwich for each of us; but I felt that it was safe to act naturally. It was ten o'clock and this was the first time we had sat down since leaving the dinner-table at eight-thirty the night before. We were feeling the strain. Earlier, in the train, I had watched both Boyd and Miles wilt and go grey, and my hip was troubling me a good deal. Whilst at the main station Miles had said as he passed: 'My God, Jim, you look terrible! Pull yourself together.' When we met again I said. 'The next time you pass a mirror have a good look at yourself.' The truth was that we were all feeling it.

A few minutes before ten-thirty we passed through the barrier and went on board the rickety little train of five or six partly-filled carriages, and punctually at the half-hour we left the station. There was still no sign of Boyd and Combe. We began to fear for their safety, but there was nothing we could do. We ran out of the city into very beautiful country with the sun shining brightly. I enjoyed that part of our journey, and the fact that we were sitting instead of standing added to my pleasure. We reached Como at five minutes to twelve, just about the time when we thought the hunt would be really up. I would not have been surprised if the station had bristled with police; but all was quiet and peaceful.

Reg went down to the exit while I waited at the rear of the train, but as Boyd and Combe did not appear I went down and joined him, surrendering our tickets.

All hope of meeting them now left us and we determined to do the best we could for ourselves. We walked straight down to the lakeside and along the waterfront to the left. Already it was hot and we felt the weight of our heavy clothes.

There were crowds of people about; but nobody took any notice of us and we soon became accustomed to passing soldiers and police without the least tremor. The road left the lakeside and passed through a residential area. Here a minor calamity befell me. The lace handle of my bag broke and the bag fell on the footpath. When I retrieved it a red gush of liquid poured out – my wine. I hastily opened the bag, heaved the broken bottle over somebody's fence and went on again. We were to feel the loss later.

The road from Como to Chiasso, the frontier town about five miles farther on, rises steadily for some kilometres, then goes steeply upward. Rich villas with lovely gardens stand on either side. On this hot day the road felt like an oven. Just as we left Como a party of police and soldiers met us in the narrowest part of the street, and passed on. Miles was keen on taking the road towards Chiasso, then leaving it as early as possible and going south up on to the San Fermo Pass in preference to going up the lakeside, and then striking due west as we had intended. I agreed; to the south the houses ceased earlier and it seemed imperative that we should get off the public highway at the earliest possible moment. So we toiled up the hill until a kilometre peg told us we were close to Chiasso; then we took a road going off in our direction, to our great relief leaving habitation behind. We crossed the railway and laboured up the hill, very conscious that if anyone behind us was looking we were visible from the toes up. A boy cyclist taking a corner with his hands off the handlebars nearly sent us flying; but his cheerful whistling was encouraging.

At last we found a deep gully which ran under the road. This was what we needed and at once we jumped into it and became partly covered in the abundant bushes. We climbed for a half-mile or so and decided to stop and eat while there was a little water still available to help wash down our tinned beef. Then we made for the hilltop, from which we could look down in almost every direction. It was a remarkable view and anxious though we were to get on, we rested a little and enjoyed the scene. Far below was Como deep in its basin at the end of the lake. I remembered reading how Garibaldi, after forced marching from Varese, had fought his way up the San Fermo Pass and halting with his men had looked down into Como. It must have been on this spot, for the road was just a little below us. We could see the lake for some distance, bordered on this side by great villas. Above the town a funicular railway ran up to a mountain village, while away to the south and south-west the great plain of Lombardy spread like a carpet.

A deep valley running from Chiasso to Lugano separated us from the snow-covered mountains, reminding us of our own Alps at the other side of the world. In the valley, road and railway ran up towards Lugano; on the other side we could trace a straight line from the snow down to the railway – the frontier fence and beyond it Switzerland.

We moved along the ridge from cover to cover, praying that no one would see us from the buildings on the mountain-side, which looked like Italian barracks. By mid-afternoon we were still obliged to advance cautiously because of the poor cover. The thin, scrubby trees were sparse and leafless as yet, and the brambles that comprised the only real vegetation did not conceal us. Deciding to rest, we dug shallow trenches with the trowel, covering ourselves with dead leaves and trying to sleep; but it was of no use. Before starting we had determined that if we were ever in doubt as to the proper course to follow we would push on, and although we were tired we soon got up and went ahead. We came to a clearing crossed by a road; beyond that was a high wood-covered peak which we made for. We nearly ran into a party of men repairing an electric power pole; veering off to avoid them brought us much too close to a farmhouse where a man was outside chopping wood. We realized very acutely that our bags looked out of place on a mountain.

Then began the ascent. All the way up, whenever I

looked back, I could see the axeman watching us intently. We walked as quickly as we could until we reached the woods, perspiring freely in the great heat. And then, as we lay resting in the shade, a gun fired from the direction of Como. 'The alarm!' we said on the instant; but other guns following reassured us. Surely they wouldn't waste all that powder on us.

By this time we were high up, and the compass showed we were south-east of Chiasso station, which we could see quite plainly. According to the map we had to get round to the south-west. We got on to a long ridge and moved very carefully at no more than a half mile an hour. By five o'clock we were due south of Chiasso, looking straight into it. We found some deep trenches half full of leaves and settled in for another meal; but we had no water and only one orange between us, so we gave up the attempt. Once we heard voices nearby and went to earth under the leaves until their owners passed. Then we had a second scare. A siren blew, filling the valley; but after a while we concluded it might have been a factory knocking off work.

At seven-thirty we came to the edge of the sparse woods and looked down into a deep valley lying athwart our course. Another wood-covered hill beyond looked forbiddingly steep and high. The valley was almost completely bare; every tree and bush had been cleared away, and occasional trenches on the hilltops suggested that it was used for the purpose of giving a field of fire. By that time we were terribly thirsty and looked longingly on a square water-hole far below us. The water gleamed in the setting sun. We were very much tempted. Fortunately our attention was distracted by the sight of distant huts and men around them; then a party of men marched in single file along the hillside. When they were met by another party, and each turned back on its tracks, we concluded that they must be the frontier patrols.

There was no sign of a fence anywhere, and after a long watch we decided that the mountain ahead was Olimpino and that the fence ran behind it. There was nothing for it but to wait until darkness and endeavour to get forward between the two patrol areas. Never was there such a leisurely sunset. It may have been beautiful; we were in no state to notice. The reluctant sun hung in the sky, a ball of fire refusing to go down.

Twilight came at last and with it the lights of Switzerland. The bright lights of the railway station and the towns and villages distinguished the neutral state from the state of war. We had not seen a lighted town since Capetown in 1940 and it was a revelation. I wanted to push on towards it when it was almost dark; but Reg wisely insisted on another hour's delay.

At last we went down, straight for the water-hole. Reg had his enamel mug ready and dipped it in. When he raised it something scrambled out – a frog! The hole was stagnant.

The going was rough. We seemed to haves got into a narrow rocky defile where the noise of our boots on the stones reverberated alarmingly. Worse still, the reflection from the lights of Chiasso flooded the whole area. For the first time stout-hearted Miles became afraid. He whispered that the combination of light with the dead stillness would make it impossible to avoid detection. 'Let us go back to the trenches and hope for better luck tomorrow,' he said. I reminded him of our vow to go on; besides we couldn't hang out another day without water. We had to get on. At the bottom we found a bog in which animals' feet had pressed holes. There was water in some of them, vile water certainly, but we drank it . . .

We began to climb. We crept up through very rocky ground expecting to see or hear the patrol above us, but no one appeared. Suddenly a sentry-box seemed to rise out of the ground a few yards in front. For a while I stalked it; but seeing and hearing nothing, walked in and inspected. No one there, and no telephone. We saw a square stone a few feet above ground and Reg went over to examine it. The next moment the world was full of the sound of bells. We fled. Thirty yards downhill we crept into a small cave under a rock, pulling our coats over us for cover. Nothing happened. Reg thought he must have struck a trip-wire with his boot. We decided to go back and explore.

We were still under the impression that the frontier

was over the hill. We crept back past the sentry-box. While Reg went up to examine a long pole that was set at an angle against a heavy post, I lay and looked upward to get a view against the light of the sky. At once the truth dawned on me – this was the frontier. The fence was not barbed-wire but high netting, fully twelve feet high and of heavy calibre, tied tightly into the bank and held out from the trees by tightly strained wires so that the slightest touch would ring the bells festooned along the top. I called to Miles, but he was out of sight. I gave the fence a slight shake and he came back at the gallop . . . 'For God's sake!'

I said, 'Quick, the wire-cutters.' While I held the fence as stiff as I could he cut out a square and I bent the jagged ends to enlarge the hole.

'Get through,' said Reg. I crawled through. He passed the coats and bags up to me, then shot through like a rabbit after them. We raced up the hill into the thick forest.

'Jim, we're in Switzerland!'

I don't know how I felt. I remember uttering a little prayer of thankfulness. My heart was tight-packed with gratitude. Then I dived into my case and hauled out the three-ounce bottle of rum. We drank to our freedom. Out of a lifetime of habit I looked at my watch. It was half-past ten.

*

James Hargest returned to England in 1943 after crossing France and Spain – the highest-ranking British officer to escape successfully in either World War.

On D-Day, 6 June 1944, he landed in Normandy as the New Zealand observer with the 30th (Northumbrian) Division. On 12 August 1944, he was killed by a shell-burst and buried near the little church at Roncamps in Normandy.

To the Japanese soldiers fighting in the Far East during the Second World War, capture was unthinkable; the Japanese code demanded that a soldier fight to the death. The number of Japanese prisoners taken during the war was, therefore, correspondingly far smaller than the figure for other belligerents – and most of those taken were wounded and unable to prevent themselves from falling into the enemy hands.

Once they were prisoners, however, the attitude of the average Japanese soldiers varied considerably. Many were content to sit out the war behind barbed wire; others found life as PoWs intolerable and committed suicide. Still others schemed to find ways of fighting and dying for their Emperor, whether in captivity or not – and it was this last attitude of mind which, in August 1944, led to the greatest and most terrifying mass escape in history.

5

The Big Break-Out

At evening roll-call the long lines of captured warriors stood like men carved from oak, as the camp guards checked reports and added up figures. Another day had ended in the largest Japanese PoW camp of the Second World War. It had been a day like many others – a day of dust and boredom, bounded by barbed wire and the immensity of the Australian plain.

Now, with their long shadows lying on the red earth, it was time for the sullen Sons of Heaven who had blazed a path of fire and death across thousands of miles of land and ocean, to be locked in their huts for the night.

The camp commandant's voice sounded flat and tired in the dying day, as he gave the words of command. Dust puffed from their boots as the Japanese soldiers, captured in bloody combat by American and Australian infantry in New Guinea and the Pacific Islands, turned and obeyed.

Not by the flicker of an eye, the twitch of a lip or a sideways glance towards the guards of Cowra Camp, New South Wales, did any prisoner drop a hint of the horror that was about to break loose over the peaceful Australian countryside.

The Japanese filed into their wooden barracks, and dusk dropped over the clump of giant gum trees, and softened the ugly outlines of barbed wire and watch-towers. Silence gradually enfolded the camp.

It was not the silence of sleep, however. Rather, on this evening of 5 August 1944, was it the stillness of a thousand men holding their breath – and waiting.

For this was D Day for the Japanese of Cowra Camp – the day for which they had worked and planned for months. The moment was at hand when they would keep their vow and wipe out, with blood, the disgrace which stained their 'honour as soldiers of the Emperor'. Their disgrace – according to the Japanese warrior code – consisted in having been taken prisoner. It made no difference that nearly all the enemy prisoners in Cowra had been wounded when they were captured.

Around the perimeter of the silent camp, rifles slung over their shoulders, the Australian guards patrolled, the crunch of their boots on gravel carrying harshly through the darkness.

Squatting in the watch-towers, other 'Diggers' shivered in their greatcoats. It was winter in the Southern Hemisphere, and the night was cold. Frost glinted under the rising moon.

Behind their machine-gun on the northern edge of the camp, Private Ben Hardy and two fellow guards turned up their collars, rubbed their hands together and longed for cigarettes.

No one suspected as the minutes ticked away, that death was creeping closer, or that the most fantastic PoW revolt of the Second World War was about to burst in Cowra Camp.

No one knew that the Japanese, outwardly so docile, so apparently broken in spirit, had collected a mass of weapons and hidden them under the floorboards of their huts – and that now most of the prisoners were armed with knives, lovingly ground to razor-sharpness, baseball bats and heavy clubs.

*

Only the Japanese held the secret of the previous night's meeting, when their leaders had slunk from their huts and wriggled through the shadows for a final conference.

It was then that the Japanese had received the last, astonishing orders – 'Kill and be killed.'

Now everything was prepared. The weapons had been issued, and the break-out shock battalion pulled on gloves and padded-clothing made from blankets. They were ready to attack the barbed wire.

With knives and clubs clutched in their hands the Japanese, huddled in their huts, began to pray – the Shinto prayer of those about to die.

For a while the muttered devotions of the stony-faced men whispered around the huts, and then they died away. And as they died, the fire began.

At first, it was just a finger of orange flame, stroking the side of a hut and blossoming into a blaze; then, as the hut burned with fiercely-growing intensity, flames began spurting from another and yet another of the wooden barracks in the prison compound.

In his white-painted home, two-hundred yards from the barbed wire of the compound, Mr Leonard Smith, manager of the Cowra Soil Conservation Station, settled down to sleep. The war news on the radio had been hopeful, he thought. Perhaps it would soon be over. Still, he thought, it hadn't disturbed life in Cowra very much . . .

In the officers' mess of an infantry training camp eight miles away, Lieutenant Harry Doncaster drank beer with three brother officers. Muted, late-night dance music filtered from the radio. The lieutenant was bored, for the war seemed very far away . . .

In the cosy bedroom of her farmstead home at nearby Bumbaldry, eight-year-old Shirley Bryant slept the dreamless sleep of childhood. For her, the war was only something that grown-ups talked about, not half so important as the new puppies which had arrived two days before. Still, she had heard of the Japanese that so many Australians were away fighting, and sometimes she wondered what one would look like . . .

Soon she would find out. The war, which had been waged far away in New Guinea and the Pacific Islands, was to come frighteningly to her peaceful home.

For now, as the fires took hold, shooting spears of light into the surrounding darkness, a thousand Japanese prisoners burst from their huts into the compound. They were not as they had been a few hours before. The shame of their captivity, endured in silence for months, had become anger which had developed into a passion to avenge their honour.

Now that passion was transmitted into madness, as screamed orders swung them into tightly-packed ranks.

Around the perimeter of the camp, searchlight beams sprang out of the night, pivoting around the compound, flickering over the burning huts, and then coming to rest on the Japanese column moving against the wire.

*

The startled Australian soldiers on the watch-towers saw, bathed in the searchlight beams, the most savage sight of the war in the Pacific. As the Japanese surged forward they appeared more like maddened animals than men. A deep baying sound rose from their ranks, and their weapons were waved above their heads as they charged towards their first objective – the machine-gun behind which Private Ben Hardy crouched.

For an instant the camp guards were too astonished to move; then a sergeant's order boomed out.

'Fire, you fools!' he barked. 'Stop them reaching the wire!'

A machine-gun on the western side of the camp began to chatter, stopped, and then began again. Tracer bullets flickered like fire-flies through the smoke and dust raised by the charging prisoners.

Some of the Japs began to fall; but the crumpled bodies might have been bundles of rags for all the notice the running men took of their fallen comrades. They swept on, packed together, almost stumbling over each other in their relentless charge. The first of them reached the inner wire.

Heavy rifle-fire, from guard posts on the fringe of the camp, began cutting into the screaming tide of humanity as it surged on to the wire.

Many men died, hung over its strands like some grotesque parody of a First World War Western Front attack; but the others, led by those with paddle clothing, pressed forward, climbing and crawling their way through.

Now they were within sight of Private Hardy's gun. The Japanese had good reason for attacking it. The break-out leaders had calculated that the gun post was in direct line of fire from other machine-guns surrounding the camp. As they got nearer to it, they believed that the gun crews would have to stop firing for fear of hitting their own men; but the firing kept up, and the 'Banzai' yells of scores of assaulting prisoners gurgled away into dying moans. Blood was now soaking the red earth of Cowra.

By this time the moonlight, cut frequently by fleeting clouds and the crimson glare of the burning huts, revealed in the compound of the camp a scene which might have been some medieval painter's vision of hell. Yet, still the attack came on.

Private Hardy's fingers tightened on the trigger of his gun and bullets spat into the figures swarming on the wire.

More than five-hundred were in this assault. The first rank melted away like a breaking wave, but those behind leapt over the bodies of their slain comrades.

Now the Japanese spread out into an encircling movement, and Hardy, wild-eyed, swung his gun. More prisoners fell, but already many of them were over the wire – and Private Hardy knew that he was doomed.

His gun was going to be overwhelmed, and when that happened one thing was sure – the Japanese would swiftly turn it against the troops guarding the camp and many more of his comrades would die.

With the maddened prisoners only a few yards away, Hardy stopped firing, snatched the breech-block from the weapon and flung it high and far into the darkness of the trees.

A few seconds later the suicide charge had engulfed him and his two comrades. The Japanese clubs rose and fell, knives flashed and stabbed, and soon the three Australians lay dead.

Yelling now with triumph, some of the escaping prisoners attempted to bring the gun into action against the watch-towers; but without the breech-block it would not fire. Private Hardy's last fight had been well fought.

Still the Japanese attack was not over. More than two-hundred prisoners stormed forward in a hopeless assault on the garrison quarters. They were stopped by deadly rifle and automatic fire. Only then did the remnants swing away and join comrades pouring over the wire to freedom.

The freedom that many of them won was the freedom of death, however. The guns kept firing, and more than twenty huts, blazing like huge bonfires, lit up the camp and its surroundings with a brilliant light. The glare illuminated the Japanese clearly, as they ran stumbling across Len Smith's paddock. Many more fell, and bullets smacked into Mr Smith's white painted house.

At last the panting survivors, some of them wounded, reached the dark line of bush and plunged into cover. The most fanatical troops of the Second World War were on the loose in a white community – the mass break-out of Cowra camp had been accomplished.

*

The cost in life had been enormous, for as the escapers streamed away into the darkness, they left more than two-hundred of their comrades dead and wounded inside the encircling wire. Bodies lay heaped in front of Private Hardy's gun. They strewed the compound in still mounds, and here and there a wounded man twitched and moaned.

The night's horror at Cowra was not yet over. As the Australians moved in cautiously towards the scene of carnage, half a dozen wounded Japanese, their way of escape cut off, flung themselves into burning huts to die in the flames.

The terror which had begun at Cowra Camp was moving on, out into the quiet farmlands. Mr Smith, roused from his bed by the first shots, crouched in a flower-bed by his garden fence, and watched as the Japanese surged past.

Later, he described the scene.

'It was like a nightmare,' he said. 'Machine-guns seemed to be firing all around. I could see the Japs running. A lot of them were falling. Sometimes they would get up and go on a little way, and then go down again. It was hard to believe that it was happening right here in my own backyard.'

Sixty-seven dead Japanese were afterwards found in his paddock.

The night wore on, and in Cowra Camp the burning huts crumbled into smouldering embers. The dead lay where they had fallen, but the wounded were picked up and carried away.

Somewhere, far off in the fields behind the garrison quarters, dogs began to howl.

In Canberra, the Australian capital, a hundred miles away to the south, a telephone shrilled on the desk of a dozing duty officer. Sleepily the lieutenant picked it up – and suddenly stiffened into wakefulness as the message came through: 'The Japs are loose.'

Within minutes, wires were buzzing to Service Chiefs. In Royal Australian Air Force squadrons, pilots were aroused and briefed to take off at first light to hunt the fugitives.

At this time, only one thing was known for certain, that hundreds of Japanese were roaming through the bush, and might already be creeping up on isolated farms and villages.

Next came the Army's turn. Soon trucks, carrying more than a thousand troops, were rumbling through the darkness. Their orders were brief: 'Get the Japs!'

Among the troops was Lieutenant Harry Doncaster. He had finished his beer in the mess, and gone to bed – only to be awakened by an excited orderly sergeant. He flicked on the light as the NCO explained: 'It's the Japs, sir! They're out!'

The war which, only a little while ago, had seemed so remote, had moved very close. Yet when Lieutenant Doncaster led his platoon out that morning, all was still peaceful. Dawn was coming, and the high, Australian sky, arching over the plains, was the colour of skimmed milk. Dew shone on the soldiers' boots as they brushed through the grass.

The patrol tramped on, every now and then spreading out to comb some thick patch of scrub. They found nothing.

*

By noon, the sweating soldiers had reached a ridge of high ground known as Boyd's Hill. All was still quiet, and it seemed a good opportunity to brew tea and eat their rations. The order to 'fall out' was given, and the troops sprawled on the grass.

Lieutenant Doncaster decided to go on a reconnaissance – alone. He skirted the side of the hill and then, walking swiftly, plunged down through a curtain of bush that masked the grassy hollow. It was there that he saw the Jap. The man was kneeling, and kindling a fire. By his side lay a skinned rabbit.

Lieutenant Doncaster broke into a run, and the PoW looked up like a startled animal. Already he had paid for his few hours of liberty with weariness, hunger and fear. He turned as though to make off as the tall Australian loped forward, calling on him to stop.

Suddenly, a cry broke from the Jap's throat. It was almost the last sound that Lieutenant Doncaster was to hear. For the fugitive was still standing with his mouth gaping when more than a dozen of his comrades erupted from the scrub. They carried stones, and they reached the Australian while his .38 Smith and Wesson revolver was still in its holster. He never had a chance to draw it. The Japanese were on him like a wolf pack and he was beaten to death.

One of the escaped prisoners took the pistol and ammunition, and then the Japs vanished into the bush.

As the hours ticked by, RAAF fighters swooped over the plains startling the grazing sheep, but their pilots saw little. The Japanese had been taught how to hide from hostile aircraft, and kept under cover.

Across the countryside, rumours flew almost as fast as the planes: 'The Japs are killing and women have been attacked.'

As darkness fell, families left isolated homesteads and moved in with neighbours. Men built huge fires to prevent surprise attack, and stood guard with shotguns.

*

Vigilante companies were organized, and mounted-scouts patrolled the high ground to give warning of marauding bands of Japanese. Australia, in 1944, was held by the kind of terror which had gripped the Old West during the Indian Wars.

The first Japanese to be retaken was found in the bush less than a mile from Cowra Camp. He was wounded, but as members of a search party went forward to pick him up, they stopped – horrified. The Jap had calmly drawn a knife, and then cut his stomach open. He was dying when the Australians reached him.

A little later, two fugitives were sighted by forty-eight-year-old locomotive engineer Mr Sam Nolan, as he drove his train along a string-straight stretch of track at Westville, eight miles from Cowra.

The Japanese stood together beside the line as the train drew near; then, when it was only three-hundred yards away, they calmly lay down on their backs across the rails. The locomotive and carriages rolled over them.

A white-faced Mr Nolan made his report to Cowra police.

'I could hardly believe what I saw. The train was doing about fifty miles an hour. There was nothing I could do.'

Three miles to the south, at about the same time, a farmer and his teenage son were out hunting hares. They stumbled on a party of fifteen Japanese squatting around a fire. One of them jumped up and rushed, screaming, at the man and boy. The farmer shot him dead. The other Japanese fled.

Next day, the second since the mass escape, hunger drove more of the Japanese towards farms and villages.

Mr Cecil Read, of Packs Grant, opened the door of a shed and found two of them milking one of his cows. He kept them covered until a truckload of soldiers drove up.

The officer-in-charge ordered the farm to be searched, and the troops began combing the outbuildings. They found a third Japanese behind the fowl-house – hanging by his neck. Besides him was a fourth, also dead. He had cut his throat.

On the same morning, sheep rancher Mr Walter Weir of Rosedale, near the little town of Holmwood, tucked a.44 rifle under his arm and stepped onto his front porch. As he closed the door behind him, a Japanese sergeant sprang from the rose bushes. Mr Weir levelled his gun.

'Hands up!' he ordered.

The Jap paid no attention, but stood quite still in front of the Australian; then he bowed slightly, slowly raised his right hand and pointed at his heart.

'Shoot here, please,' he pleaded.

When Mr Weir refused, tears ran down the man's face. Police took him away.

*

Driven by growing fears of a massacre, if gangs of Japanese should attack homesteads, the search for them developed in scope and intensity.

The pilot of one aircraft saw twenty of the fugitives with a sheep they had killed. He radioed for a mobile column of troops. The Japanese surrendered quietly and were marched off, their heads bowed in shame.

Although hunger was weakening the PoWs, it was a

factor that added to the dangers facing the farmers and their families. The Japanese had to eat, and farms were the only places where food was to be found.

Little Shirley Bryant was feeding lambs in the back-yard of her home, when she saw her first Japanese. A thick-set man, his face caked in blood from a wound in his brow, his uniform filthy and in tatters, and his eyes staring, crawled from a hedge and moved towards her.

Shirley's green eyes grew wide and she stood gazing at the shambling figure of the enemy soldier; then, as the Jap came closer with hands outstretched, her face crumpled. She broke into sobs, dropped her feeding bowl and turned and ran, calling for her mother.

The PoW ran, too; but he was still a few paces behind the child when Mrs Bryant slammed the door of her home behind her daughter and turned the key.

When she looked out of the window, the Jap was standing in the yard. He was holding a knife, and he pointed to his mouth.

'Bread, bread!' he repeated.

Mrs Bryant threw him half a loaf. He snatched it up and walked away.

At Woodstock, twelve miles distant, Mrs Winifred Clarke came around the corner of her house and saw six Japanese, all carrying clubs, crouching beside the water tank. She locked her eight children in the living-room, and ran two-hundred yards to the police station;

but when an armed sergeant arrived the PoWs had vanished.

They were rounded up an hour later.

That evening, the telephone rang in the home of Mr Ronald McDiarmid, five miles from Cowra. A neighbour gave him a message.

'Twenty Japanese are heading your way,' was the warning.

Mr McDiarmid bolted his doors, and snatched up a rifle; then he saw the escaped prisoners forming up in two groups behind his house.

Were they going to attack? For a moment, it looked as though they would; but suddenly they turned away.

Next morning, Mr McDiarmid found six of them, dead or dying, less than a hundred yards from his home. They had committed suicide by cutting their throats or stabbing themselves in the body.

By this time, the fugitives were desperately weak with hunger and thirst. A large party of them waved to a truck-driver on a road south of Cowra. He drove on into town and troops went and brought the Japs in.

Two days later, the great break-out was over. The last of the Japanese had been rounded-up or had surrendered. Eight more committed suicide.

*

It was time to bury the dead. This was done in secret. The bulldozer scooped out eight mass graves in the red earth of Cowra and then, at night, the bodies of two hundred and thirty Japanese soldiers, who had taken part in the strangest and most bloody prison break of the war, were brought in carts and trucks to be buried.

By the flickering light of burning oil torches, and the glare of truck headlights, Australian troops unloaded piles of corpses and dumped them in the graves.

There was no burial ceremony. Armed military patrols, and barbed-wire road-blocks made certain that nobody but the working parties reached the cemetery.

Only one more thing remained to be said about the great break-out from Cowra Camp. A grey-faced Japanese, being interrogated next day, said it to an interpreter, as he stood once more within the encircling wire.

'Why should I mourn?' he asked. 'When a soldier of Japan is taken prisoner, he is officially regarded as dead. Now my comrades are buried. Before the break-out, they walked and talked; but they were dead then – even as I am today.'

Richard Pape was a Sergeant Navigator who was shot down and captured in 1941 while returning from a raid on Berlin. Inspired by Douglas Bader to escape at all costs, he made persistent attempts to regain his freedom. This is the story of one of them, made while Pape was an inmate of the notorious Stalag VIIIB *in Upper Silesia.*

6

Boldness Be My Friend

The Pole and I were detailed to work in a tortuous tunnel which rose and fell for the best part of a mile. Its average height was five feet. Branching off from it were scores of other passages and from these, many other offshoots and forkings. Had it been possible to look downwards with X-ray eyes, the workings of the Hohenzollern coalmine would have resembled the vein formation of a leaf.

For more than sixty years this veteran Obersilesian pit had yielded a continuous output of rich coal from its three separate levels. Hundreds of miles of tunnel had been hacked out between rock layers in all directions, extending for miles around the pivot point of the shaft's base.

Our tunnel was two and a half miles from the cage, but fate favoured our escape plans by directing us to work in this remote section of the pit. In this easterly underground location there were many gangs of Polish miners in the adjacent labyrinth of tunnels.

Mieteck's job was rail laying, and this gave him a first-class opportunity to meet them. His masquerade as a New Zealand private soldier was carefully maintained, and whenever he was compelled to open his mouth he spoke in English or halting German. At every possible opportunity he listened to his countrymen and their whispered conversations, watchfully assessing every man. Eventually he was certain that a certain man was trustworthy and would help us when our story was revealed.

Mieteck's choice was a middle-aged Polish miner, who, we learned, was a key man against German interests. To all outward appearances, he was a model worker, but Mieteck had observed from careful judgement that he was some kind of secret leader who stealthily imparted orders and information to selected Poles.

After the day's work, Mieteck would relate to me all that he had picked up while laying his rails. He had learned of a great many things connected with activities against the Germans, and German atrocities against the Poles. After a couple of weeks of such listening, I noticed that Mieteck returned to his bed dreadfully upset and unusually quiet. Somehow I sensed that he was slipping. He was in a terrible situation, a fugitive and an imposter in his own land and among his own countrymen; but patience and diplomacy were vital. I had to pitch into Mieteck many times when in despair he told me that he intended to reveal his nationality and talk in the Polish language.

'Watch and wait,' I told him. 'For God's sake don't go and spoil everything for a ha'porth of impatience. The snow in Poland is still too thick and the weather too foul for an immediate and successful escape. Wait a while longer for the quick thaw, and then tell your story to these countrymen of yours. As long as you are master of our secret, we're masters of the situation.'

I sincerely felt that if Mieteck revealed his true identity prematurely, the sudden companionship and inevitable excitement it would cause underground might well lead to disaster. I sympathized with, and consoled him about the tragedies of his people; but I cherished in my mind only one thought: avoid all sentiment and sentimentality to achieve one purpose.

It was now obvious to me that Mieteck possessed some kind of a dual personality. He was tough, brave, reliable and determined away from Poland; but on his own stamping ground his spirits tended to oscillate widely and unpredictably.

My work at the coalface was more severe than my companions. Throughout the long shift I shovelled coal into wagons with two Poles, three Russians and a Frenchman. Four Germans supervised the explosive blasting and the erection of the pine props. At the start the heavy work contracted my back, arm and leg muscles into knots, but once stiffness had worn away, the continuous daily labour tempered my limbs and muscles into flexible steel, in spite of inadequate food. My body gained in wiry strength week after week: good preparation for the big escape.

I was involved in one bad mishap. Towards the end of a shift, just after the German in charge had detonated his explosive and loosened a quantity of coal, a shower of heavy rocks hurtled down without warning. A German had a leg broken and a shoulder fractured, a Russian had his skull fractured and two of the Poles were badly crushed. I escaped with the least injury by diving hard against a steel tub which narrowed at the base. Nevertheless, in spite of the protection from the tub's upper flange, my back was lacerated and the lower part of my spine bruised. I was taken to the hospital with the others but was discharged after only three days, the doctor informing me that I would be given a light duty voucher which would keep me on the surface for ten days.

*

During the rest from heavy underground work, I met six others who possessed light duty chits. We were assembled by the officer in charge of the slave labour, a diminutive rat of a man we nicknamed 'John the Bastard', and were told that one light duty would be among captive Russian women in the nearby briquette factory.

'You will understand', he snarled, 'that you will see all you ever want to see of half-naked women. But remember . . . that is the limit of your association with them. If you had been Germans instead of foreign pigdogs you would have been entitled to Russian flesh sport.'

Daily we marched to the briquette factory, through the strong barbed-wire fences and into the two long black sheds. Daily we stacked and trundled coal briquettes on barrows, and in the yards outside restacked them into fifteen-foot-high squares.

Within the black corrugated metal sheds laboured and perspired 200 Russian women. When their homes had been overrun and their native earth scorched by their own retreating armies; when their families had been either annihilated or hopelessly separated, the invaders had herded them into cattle trucks and brought them into Germany as slave labour. The average age of the women was about twenty-eight and, like the coal briquettes they moulded daily from pitch and coal dust, they also were moulded in a filthy and disgusting communal existence. They had to contend with harsh discipline and the unrelenting pressure of manual labour. They writhed under physical and mental starvation, and clamoured for food and friendship in a world of suffering, fear and loneliness. The younger element found lack of peace even after a day's toil, for the guards made a habit of visiting their quarters. For ten days I watched, walked and worked among these wretched women.

Inside the factory only middle-aged Germans supervised the briquette manufacture and attempted to enforce discipline. Evidently they had been specially selected. Two possessed an artificial leg apiece, while number three was bent almost double with rheumatism and apparently immune to the steaming bodies about him. His fanatical enthusiasm for greater coal briquette production for domestic German heating made him completely unsexual. But that was not quite the case with the two other guards. Both derived crude, erotic gratification through continually pinching, patting and prodding the Russian women as they moved among them. The misery of those women's lives, the privations they suffered, their unnatural segregation, their normally crude peasant make-up, created in them a feverish flood of desire for grotesque exhibitionism whenever the six young and reasonably virile Englishmen moved among them.

At first the whole set-up was repelling and obnoxious, but not for long. Close proximity became a physical torture. When would such opportunity occur again? Conscience and fear of consequences dispersed as impulses and instincts inspired the means to cheat the supervision of the guards. The German crippled with rheumatism soon became pro-British after he had been bribed with a few odds and ends of Red Cross items. He nodded acquiescence to forbidden love between the Russian women and British men, enacted behind the high stacks of coal briquettes in the yard outside.

Some of the women were tall and stooping, some revealed Mongolian features, others were short and appeared oddly misshapen in their ragged and wretched attire of unfashioned sackcloth. The boiling vats of tar and pitch stoked up the temperature, and the interior of the sheds became sticky, sickly, stifling. Heat and fumes were choking as the huge cauldrons spewed and bubbled, and oddments of sacking garments were discarded for freedom and coolness. Lack of underclothing was as common as lack of decency. Breasts and bodies were coated with shiny black coal dust, glistening and gleaming on the underlay of ever-rising sweat globules.

Over the moulds the women stooped, their swaying breasts hanging and rivulets of perspiration trickling to the floor. Faces were sullen, gaunt and vacuous, but even such cow-like expressions failed to obscure a leering lust whenever we passed them by or inadvertently contacted their hot and steaming bodies. It seemed that 200 ravenous women were magnetized by the young Englishmen. All the women knew that ways and means existed, and this made each man a hunted quarry.

In those sheds of rising and settling coal dust and heat it was a life beyond belief. Some of the women were already padded with pregnancy; those who were not begged us to fertilize them. Pregnancy meant relief. At the approach of the birth of the child the camp doctor would order the women away for light duty and prescribe for them additional rest with extra rations. That was their relief.

The Germans were anxious to increase their population, including nondescripts. Babies were placed in German state homes at the earliest date to be nurtured as cannon fodder and inculcated with the ideology of the Third Reich. The Russian women cared little what happened to the babies they bore. As far as childbirth was concerned it simply meant lighter work and a decent rest with considerably more food.

*

When the shift was over the Germans always left the mine first. Only when the last relay had been taken aloft were we allowed to move towards the cage. We squatted in weary groups at the base of the shaft, sweaty, and thick with Obersilesian coal dust, talking and patiently waiting. We represented to the Germans so many pigdog slave labourers. Successive military successes had affected queerly the civilian mentality. We were classed as so much human scum which the proud 'Wehrmacht' had passed on to them. It was the duty of the civilians to enforce duty and discipline; to do otherwise would be to oppose Nazism.

Every day as we waited for the cage I spoke with Ivanov, a young Russian with a face showing character and determination. Speaking in German, he told me about his home town of Minsk, his life, and the annihilation of his entire family. Enthusiastic and proud, he told me of Vladimir Rasumov, the finest friend in the world, the only one he honoured most next to Joseph Stalin himself. Vladimir was twenty-five years his senior, and had been the respected headmaster of one of the best schools in Minsk. Ivanov would speak of Vladimir's brain with a certain awe.

'Nobody in the whole province could approach my friend for mathematical ability, philosophy or a true knowledge of economics,' said Ivanov.

I would steal a sidelong glance at Vladimir Rasumov, hunched dejectedly against the dripping wall, emaciated, bent and dirty. The idea of associating him with scholastic achievement seemed incongruous. Schoolmaster and pupil had both been captured together, and now worked together for the Germans as human pit ponies.

'Vladimir never speaks to a soul except me,' Ivanov continued. 'Ever since he saw his wife ablaze inside his fired schoolhouse, he has remained silent.'

I tried to engage him in conversation many times, but it was hopeless. Rasumov only spoke with a look from his deep and searching eyes. In the sanctuary of his barracks, with Ivanov by his side, it was different. He became a totally changed being. He would monopolize every minute of the young man's time with deep and sober instruction. Mathematics, languages, economics and philosophy were imparted to the young Russian. The schoolmaster was fanatical in the passing on of his knowledge.

'Economics and philosophy are his favourite subjects,' Ivanov remarked. 'He maintains that only by understanding and power can political enlightenment be obtained, and a will enforced.'

Ivanov was receptive to his instruction, and I was staggered when he told me that he was up to differential 'R' in pure mathematics. He would also quote with authority from Karl Marx and Rodertus. Never had I seen an older man leave such an impression upon a younger one.

When Vladimir Rasumov was killed, it was horrible to see the young man's suffering. The frail schoolmaster had been kicked by Schmidt, the Nazi overseer, for not pushing his trucks to the shaft with greater speed. A short time later he collapsed on the line, and a heavy fast-moving wagon crushed him to death. Sympathy appeared useless, and during the ensuing days I refrained from discussing the affair. At last Ivanov regained some of his friendliness, but he made some odd remarks with a detached kind of vacancy.

'Economic blows smart longer and disrupt greater. Murder is too paltry, and synonymous of bad education,' Ivanov said contemplatively.

'What the devil?' I said to myself. 'Surely Ivanov is not crazy?'

Occasionally the continuous activities of the mine simply had to cease, and the cages and underground machinery be repaired and renewed. The next Sunday was a stand down. Shifts were always lengthened afterwards, to maintain the output. Coal was vital and fundamental for the Germans' total war, and they got it by threat, fear and explosive. It was explosive that was used to tear out the coal from between the rock layers. The safe and normal methods of production were discarded for greater production.

The day before the stand down, Ivanov asked me with studied casualness how a *Zimmer* box was connected to a charge. This instrument was the hand-operated contrivance for detonating the explosive charge by remote control. A thought struck me immediately, forcibly. '*Mein lieber Gott!*' I replied. 'Please remember all the slave labour scattered throughout the mine. Please don't do anything stupid.'

He smiled his slow odd smile. 'Stupid, my English friend? Excuse me . . . I don't think I was ever stupid. Nor will Russia ever be stupid again now that Stalin is our mentor.'

Three special roll calls were held that night by the Germans. A Russian had escaped from the top of the pit while crossing to his barracks.

A guard spat and remarked: 'Russians are so obviously

dim and stupid we can tell them anywhere. He'll get caught all right . . . he hasn't a chance.'

It was beautifully timed, an hour before the pit was due to take down its first intake. The explosion occurred 300 yards from the entrance of the main tunnel, in the passage which carried to the shaft all the coal from the many tributaries. What a blockage! Hundreds of tons of rock sealed the tunnel and crashed on the reconditioned trucks, the auxiliary air plant, and the sand-flowing tubs. It was masterly, studied, mathematical. It took two days to reorganize the routine and production was lost. It was 'economic warfare' with a vengeance! Not a single person was killed.

The Gestapo arrived in force and verified that all prisoners, with the exception of the Russian, had been checked up and safely locked away for the night under careful armed guard. Only the Russian was missing. He had been brought up in the last cage and had been seen escaping from the surface. He was never recaptured.

*

Mieteck was becoming increasingly irritable. Listening, as he did below ground, to many stories of the tragedy of Poland's plight, was, I assumed, diverting him from his own purpose and ultimate belief in victory. My policy was clear. I advanced the date of escape, disregarding the fact that the Polish plains were still snow-covered and the weather far from suitable. We would risk it, for the Pole was my most valuable escape asset.

I told Mieteck to reveal his true identity to the men he thought were genuine. It turned out that his assessments of the Poles in the workings were correct. Mieteck told them everything and they were greatly impressed. Their first act after our secret had been divulged was to kneel and pray together in the coal dust. They were all devout Catholics and many prayer sessions took place. This only tended to arouse my ire. Perhaps self-ishly, I imagined that such devotion might soften up my companion.

The Poles conspired in the bowels of the earth to good purpose. Money, maps, and clothing were produced but, most important of all, we were provided with a valuable address in Czestochowa, from which it was more than likely that we would gain entry into the Polish underground movement. The leader of the loyalist miners promised that he would contact Czestochowa, notify the underground of our probable arrival and give them our descriptions. Further, an important password would be given us before we left the mine.

Mieteck was carefully schooled about the circuitous route we would have to follow to avoid the danger spots, and a list of villages was given to us with the names of reliable helpers in each. The distance to our destination, following a roundabout route, was more than 100 kilometres. Instead of heading north-east – the nearest distance between the two points – we would set course due east towards Wolbrom, approximately fifty kilometres away. Fifteen kilometres from Wolbrom we would swing north-west and make towards Czestochowa, some sixty-five kilometres as the crow flies. The whole journey would be completed in a series of treks from village to village. We were told that it was much too risky a journey to be undertaken by train.

We had all our supplies and civilian clothes gathered together and concealed, and the escape date definitely fixed. It was to take place on my birthday. But just before our departure two other captives made a break. They were recaptured only two miles away. Under civilian police escort, they were returned to the pit head and handed over to 'John the Bastard'. Instantly, he exploded into one of his violent rages and without hesitation shot the two men dead. Even this did not appease the maniac. He ordered the two bodies to be hung in crucifixion on the barbed-wire as a stark reminder of what would happen to others who tried to escape.

'Good God.' murmured Mieteck, shaken. 'Now we know our fate if we're captured and brought back.'

'We're definitely going . . . as arranged,' I replied. 'Fate has merely given us a warning to clear this murder dump good and proper . . . and with no mistakes.' Although I was ill at ease, I was determined not to tolerate any further postponement of our escape.

Mieteck, a firm believer in silent supplication, prayed mightily. He told me sincerely that he would stab himself to death rather than give 'John the Bastard' the satisfaction of shooting him in cold blood and draping his body on the wire.

Then, two days before the date fixed for escape, fate again took a hand, but this time to our advantage. The pit authorities decided to change the time of our underground shift so that instead of escaping after our duty, tired, dirty and aching, we would now be able to move off before we went underground. We would be fresh, clean, clear thinking, and we would still have the darkness to cover our movements.

The colliery routine was this: before lining up in front of the cage each day for counting and checking, the prisoners had to march to the bath house, a large decentralized building. Here we unhooked our mining clothes and boots, helmet and lamp. After changing into underground apparel, the party reassembled in the doorway for counting. Then, satisfied that we were all present and correct, the guards marched us to the platform cage where the military guards handed us over to the civilian overseers responsible for our care and discipline underground. Before the guards moved away, a further count would take place as the prisoners entered the cages two at a time.

The critical minutes of our escape came in the ten minute interval between the pithead counts. During that time Mieteck and I had to make the break. Further, we had to cross a tricky, fortified bridge to gain the railway sidings. Once among the trucks we would be difficult to spot and hard to hit but beyond the parked wagons, half a mile from the pithead, a high wire-mesh fence surrounded the mine property. This had to be overcome before we could gain the main highway into the town and collect the bicycles which would be parked at a prearranged spot. Every moment would count until we cleared the town of Beuthen. We presumed that the Germans would fan out and search the precincts of the mine inside the wire before alerting the civilian police in the town.

Every day for a week Mieteck and I had smuggled into the bath house our escape supplies and hid them behind the built-in-lockers. On the eve of our escape we got the whole gang together and thrashed out, as scientifically as possible, the most advantageous point at which we could slip away from the column of marching men. We decided on a position midway between the bath house and the pithead, to the left of the pathway opposite a twenty-foot-high stack of pit props. The men who would be leading the column promised to veer gently towards the stack of timber and slacken speed. Two men at the front would start an argument to distract the escorting guards. The tallest men in the coalmining party would be placed to the front and left of us and behind us to act as a screen.

When the morning came snow was falling gently. This was Heaven's own birthday present. I was also touched by Mieteck's gift to me: a crucifix on a thin chain. It was a fine and thoughtful gesture.

As we walked to the bath house I asked Mieteck how he was feeling.

'Don't worry,' he replied. 'We'll make it. I feel it in my heart. But please don't swear so furiously if we encounter any obstacles.'

Mieteck never swore, and it was only at this important hour that I realized that my ripe language was distasteful to my religious Polish companion.

'I'll try not to,' I replied, sincerely. 'But just as you derive moral support from a nice quiet prayer, I get similar satisfaction from a good round of swearing. It does me good. It's only a habit.'

The guards took up their accustomed position at the door. The men primed to assist us safely covered us from suspicious eyes as Mieteck and I quickly donned the pit dress over our escape suits, collected our supplies and, with helmets on heads and knapsacks pressed tightly to our sides, took up our prearranged positions. The guards counted the men, noticed nothing unusual, and gave the command to march. The column of prisoners crunched ahead and, like a frontier box between heaven and hell, the black bulk of stacked pit props loomed before us through the falling snow.

The two prisoners in front, a man called Burns and

a little Cornishman, began their shindy with gusto. The guards rushed forward. Now the wood pile was opposite me. Ducking, I threw myself flat at the base of the stack. The instant my face touched the snow, Mieteck sprawled on top of me. We lay still. The rest of the party crunched ahead into the veil of falling snowflakes. I heard the angry voice of Bums threatening to kick the Cornish-man in the ruddy guts.

The narrow bridge we had to cross was forty feet to the left of the woodpile. It spanned an eight-feet-wide cutting in which were stationed strings of railway trucks awaiting their turn to be loaded at the bunkers with coal. It was a good forty-feet drop from the bridge to the trucks below. The bridge, four feet wide, was of steel girders and guarded by a high, flat, steel door which was always kept locked. To make the barrier additionally escape-proof, the Germans had extended high steel plates eight feet to the left and right of the doorway, presumably to prevent unauthorized persons from clambering around the locked door and jumping over the bridge's parapet. But that was not all. Barbed-wire stretched in rows from where the plates ended to points ten feet out on the parapet. The only way out of the mine was to swing along the barbed wire to the parapet. Our only protection against the worst tearing of the barbs was leather-faced mittens. There was no support for our feet and, forty feet below, were the loaded wagons.

Mieteck was first over. He gripped the wire and flung himself outwards, grappling and tearing his way across. The wire squeaked, groaned and sagged but he reached the parapet safely and pulled himself over.

As soon as his weight was off the wire I, too, gripped it and swung outwards. Every second counted. Mieteck's weight had loosened the wire appreciably and my own heavier weight and forceful wriggling made it slacker and slacker. I found it impossible to get over at anything like the same speed. The wire barbs hooked into my chest and I was compelled to jerk and wriggle alarmingly to release myself. It was sickening to feel my feet kicking at nothing. And I dared not wrench and heave too violently or I would have left most of my clothing behind.

I was spreadeagled on the strands no more than two-thirds of the way across when a series of yells told me that our disappearance had been discovered. This wire business had taken longer than anticipated. Oh Christ! What a corner we were in.

Searchlights from the main tower switched on. One swept around wildly, the other centred its beam smack in the middle of the bridge. Demoniacally, I writhed, wrenched, tugged, and released myself for the twentieth time. I crabbed along in a muck sweat. And then, even as Mieteck reached over and helped me across the parapet, footsteps raced along the pathway leading to the bridge.

Without a second's hesitation I bent double and hurtled forward, my head just lower than the steel rail parapet, Mieteck on my heels. All fear and hesitation were gone. Over the eighty feet of wooden boards we streaked, our pounding boots kicking up a hellish clatter, as we hurtled through the white cone of the searchlight.

At the barbed wire the pursuing Germans halted and opened fire with their sub-machine-guns. But now the locked steel door and protruding steel walls that had barred our way came to our aid. The guards were compelled to aim on the angle. Had they been able to shoot straight up between the parapets it would have been certain death for us both.

Bullets pinged and spewed around us as we clanged down the metal steps at the other end. In the glow of a small pilot lamp at the bottom stood a watchman with arms outstretched. I was still in the lead and, taking a spring from the last few steps above the ground I neatly contacted the man's crutch with my boot. Every ounce of my strength went into the kick and he dropped like a log.

We cleared the lines of coal trucks, weaving in and out of at least half a dozen separate sidings, and gained the open. We raced the remaining 300 yards to the mesh fence. It was twelve feet high and so finely woven that there was no grip anywhere. With lungs almost at bursting point we followed the fence towards the main road.

Sucking and gulping for breath, I reached into my haversack for a metal hook and rope which would overcome this last barrier.

It was not there. We must have left it in the bath house.

Mieteck said never a word, but he ran up and down inside the wire like a mad dog. My heart pounded hysterically. To climb the mesh fence was impossible. It was all my fault, and in the turmoil of mental agony I could not think what to do. Mieteck was now out of sight, and I thought he had deserted me. Then I heard him call, and raced up to him. He was on his knees, tearing away at the earth with his knife.

'Help me! Help me!' he sobbed. 'Dig! Dig!'

Here the base of the mesh fence was on sloping ground and revealed a five-inch clearance. With fanatical energy we ripped out enough of the hard earth to allow a belly wriggle under the wire. With incredible speed it was accomplished and one after the other we crawled through.

On the other side we took off our pit helmets and buried them, putting our civilian felt hats on in their place. Then we turned our backs on our prison.

We had made it.

*

After a gruelling trek through snow and freezing cold, Pape was eventually recaptured and flung into a political prison near Cracow, where he was tortured by the Gestapo. Yet again he escaped and was recaptured. Finally, in April 1944 – while in Stalag Luft VI *– he managed to convince his captors that he was suffering from an advanced kidney disease by swallowing pieces of soap. The ruse was good enough to hoodwink both the German doctors and a repatriation board, and in September 1944 Pape returned to England via Sweden.*

A Sergeant in the 2nd Glosters, Douglas Collins was taken prisoner at Dunkirk. During the next four years he made no fewer than ten escape attempts, usually with his friend, Edward Lancaster. The following chapter tells of his eighth escape, on this occasion from Lagarul 14 PoW *camp in Romania.*

7

Romanian Adventure

On the evening of the 17th the camp was quiet. Everyone knew the attempt was to be made within an hour and the knowledge would not be ignored. It sat on the mind like a weight. Outside, the mood was matched by an overcast sky.

The escapers had made preparations and said their farewells. Roll call, now that night fell early, had been already held. All we had to do was to go. Packs were stacked in the tunnel room and the prisoners sat at their bean supper, saying little.

Garrett came over to where I was sitting with Ted and asked whether things were OK.

'They need livening up a bit,' I told him, and caught myself whispering. 'We're much too quiet. Let's be normal. Get the guys shouting.'

Limey jumped up, uttering, 'To hell with Romania!'

Somebody chased out into the kitchen, yelling at the top of his voice, and soon the usual pandemonium reigned.

'They all know what to do,' said Garrett. 'There'll be just two of us watching what goes on. The rest stay in here or in their rooms, and once you're out we'll start singing. That'll cover any noise you make.'

Keeping away from the windows was important. It wouldn't do to have a gallery peering. The guards might start peering, too.

Of the original sixteen, eight had opted out. It had always been stressed that anyone who was not happy about the operation should say so, and the ones who quit did so without embarrassment. But they had all continued working on the tunnel and one of them had volunteered to break surface for us. He was a youngster of nineteen named Arthur White, and now he came back, ashen-faced.

'Dammit, Mac, It's like daylight out there.'

'What d'you mean?'

'I mean you guys'll never make it. The lamps are shining right down on the hole.'

By our reckoning the tunnel exit should have been in shadow. It was an error that rose before us like a rock.

'But we're coming out right where we thought we would. About five yards from the fence. And that's where the light falls off.'

'Well it ain't fallin' off tonight. I'm tellin' you.'

'How far are we from the fence?'

'Far enough. I didn't stick my top up that much. You might just as well wave at the guards. You guys would be better off to hold on for a while. Stick some earth on boards and make it look like nothing happened. Then you can drive the hole farther.'

'It wouldn't work. They'd spot it right away. Before breakfast, when they inspect the grounds. And to make the hole longer might take us to first snow. If we're going at all we'll have to take a chance with what we've got.'

The others were waiting in the tunnel room. We joined them and gave them the story.

'We're going ahead unless it's absolutely impossible. And there isn't much time.'

They nodded.

'Let's get moving then.'

The words came from Joe Brown, an old man of forty-three, a Chicago policeman who had served with the Marines in the Nicaraguan campaign while we were still in short pants, and who had chosen to be a policeman in Chicago. He and Rurak argued constantly about whether cops were crooked. 'Capone was never any pal of mine,' he would protest, and Rurak would hoot and say that Capone had bought the whole police force from chief to rookie. Now he and Rurak looked funny, sitting there with blackened faces and wearing their bits and pieces of uniform. We all looked funny, but no one had any decent jokes. Not even White, who usually bubbled like a hot pot, nor Harry Baughn, who was usually good for a quip, nor Limey. Ray Heisner, a dour but determined Detroiter, blinked in silent query. James Brittain, who with Lancaster and myself made up the eight in the group, said nothing.

I turned to Garrett.

'Well then, it's on.'

'Good luck.'

I took my pack and dropped into the open shaft. At first the only light that could be seen was a faint glow. But as the tunnel turned, light streamed in with a hard brightness.

I reached the exit and stopped. White had done his work well. The opening gaped wide and getting out of it would not be difficult provided there was no alarm. But that seemed too much to hope for because from this worm's eye view the sky looked like pre-war Piccadilly.

Feeling a little foolish I raised my battered hat on a stick the way the cowboys do it in the movies. Nothing happened, and in the centre of my fear I felt disappointment. If a bullet had crashed into the night, face would have been saved and the effort would have been over. Now I would have to go on. National pride would not let me go back to the Americans and make excuses. England expects . . . and what was far worse now was that America was expecting. I thought of Limey and his lop-sided grin, and pushed myself out into the open and lay prone, certain that the movement must have been seen.

The arc lamps thrust their glare directly on the wire, the outer line of which was eight to ten feet behind me. The nearest guard was at the south-east corner of the camp, about sixty feet away, where he could cover both the front of the complex and the side where the escape was taking place. Usually he looked down the road, although he had only to turn his head to scan the strands up to the south-west corner where stood guard number two. And number two was the main danger. The ground at his end rose sharply so that he dominated the scene. If we got that far we would have to crawl past him.

What were the sentries doing now? I longed to glance up but dared not. Inch by inch I wriggled forward. One yard; two yards; three. The black fence. I turned into its protective background, hardly able to believe that the game was still being played.

Face to the ground, I peered under my arm to see what was happening at the tunnel. Ted was emerging, clearly visible, to me at least, although I now realized that the guards were at a disadvantage. They were in the circles of light. We, if not in shadow, were in the penumbra. To see us they would have to cast more than a casual glance.

Half-way up the fence. Three more crawling figures are now strung out behind me. A dog barks in the neighbouring grounds. It is suspicious even if the guards aren't. But the dog alerts the men and now guard number one says something and number two sends the beam of a powerful flashlight sweeping along the boards. It waves about uncertainly, missing me by a couple of feet. Surely they must have seen us? And what is Garrett doing? The camp is as quiet as a tomb and we need noise. In this stillness every sound is magnified.

As if by telepathic signal the singing begins. John Brown's body lies a-mouldering in the grave. God bless your American boots, Garrett. Now we can move again and already we're drawing near to number two and moving parallel to the wire. I stop again, sweating heavily, and see that Ted has stopped too. The whole line stops. Another chap comes out of the hole and there's a temptation to get up on one's knees and make better time. I resist it. The sentry coughs. Level with him now and he's no more than five yards away. The bushes, thank Christ! Ted arrives and I grasp him by the arm. A few yards more and we stand up and move through the blackness of the trees. The ground rises steeply and below us the camp is an oasis of light.

We clamber on and up, branches whipping at our faces, but we feel nothing but elation. Nearly at the top now and the sense of awayness acts on us like a stiff drink.

In a split second we are sober again. A shot crashes out, followed by a shout and more shooting. Four shots, perhaps five.

Only one thing for it now. Run like hell. A mile away, a road circles the hill we are on, and part of the Romanian escape drill is to put troops along it to seal the area off. We must cross the road before they get there.

We reach the crest and pause for breath. Off again. I fall over a log and see stars. Ted falls too and tears his pants. He curses and we pick ourselves up. We pound away once more and burst suddenly into the open. The clouds have cleared now and the moon is up and the white surface of the gravel road stretches out like a ribbon. To make things worse there's a wide grass verge on either side of it. If the Romanians are already in position, we have had it.

'Come on,' says Ted, and moves forward. We are over in seconds and start scrambling up a hill that is twin to the one we have just come down. No sooner do we reach the trees than two trucks screech to a halt below us. Men jump from them, yelling. A volley is fired. A second one crashes out, its echoes blending in the soundbox of the mountains with those of the first. Then a burst of machine-gun fire. They are aiming blindly into our hill but their lack of vision does nothing for our morale. A burst brings down a shower of leaves and twigs on our heads.

Silence.

'You know what?' whispers Ted. 'I can hear your bloody heart beating.'

'What surprises me is that those guards down there can't hear it.'

A few more shots. None come close. The trucks are driven slowly down the road but we know that some men have been left behind to keep watch. We lie still for an hour and then get up cautiously and go on and up. We are on the right side of the Romanian ring. We are away. *Gott sei Dank*!

*

That night was spent a few miles north of the camp. The mountain morning dawned cold and from a coign on a steep cliff we could watch the main road, the same road that led past Timisul. Sometimes a truck full of troops sped by and we wondered whether they were looking for us. But there was a certain smugness in knowing that we could never be found as long as we stayed where we were. It was the kind of feeling one got as a kid playing hide-and-seek in the woods. But we could not stay here forever. We had to get to Brasov, ten miles away, and catch a train.

We munched some bread and cheese and took stock.

'Got the money?'

'Yes.'

'Wonder what happened to the others?'

'God knows. Hope nobody got hurt.'

'You know what?'

'What?'

'Being first out didn't take the guts. It's the last one who runs the risks. The last one's got to rely on all the others making no mistakes.'

'That's true if everybody's out. But if the alarm goes up and the last man hasn't started he's got no worries.'

'I doubt whether everybody got out last night.'

It is still chilly and the familiar melancholy descends. But this time we brush it off. We have the precious telephone number. What we have to do is to reach Bucharest, and for that we need luck and patience. Wait two days to let things quiet down and then walk into Brasov and make the big bid.

*

Great endeavours are often ruined by simple things. The mouse panics the elephant. And Ted's tom pants now took on the shape of disaster. His leg showed whitely through the rip, a hirsute declaration of our differentness. But we had no needle and thread.

'I'll have to go in and buy some. You can't walk through the streets like that. We'd be stared at.'

The edge of unreasonable rebuke was in my voice and Ted looked unhappy. I laughed in apology and called him a silly sod who couldn't walk straight in the dark.

It was the second day. Brasov lay before us, ghostly in the early evening. Ted stayed under cover and I set out. It would be just my luck to be caught trying to buy needle and thread, I thought. But the job turned out to be easy. There were many German-speaking Saxons in the area and the man behind the counter asked no questions. I brought some hot sausages too, and hurried back. Ted got busy on the repairs and grunted contentedly over the food.

'One more night in the woods. Then in to buy the tickets.'

In the morning we shaved in a stream and walked into the city. It was market day and the streets were full of farmers. No one took any notice of us and we got to the station without trouble. We found that the ticket office didn't open until 11 am, so the intervening two hours were spent visiting coffee shops and sitting in the darkest seats. We marched into the station separately, knowing that the police might be watching for us. It was as full as the streets. But we couldn't find what we were looking for.

Three times I tried to ask for directions; none of the people I spoke to understood German, but in the end I saw a German captain. He was obviously in transit and would not have heard about the escape. He was worth a risk.

'Können Sie mir sagen, Herr Hauptmann, wo ich mir eine Fahrkarte herkaufen kann?'*

---

*'Can you tell me where I can buy a ticket, Captain?'

He couldn't help, and called over to a German Red Cross nurse. She took her head. I was about to go when the captain spoke to a civilian and the civilian said, '*Kommen Sie mit!*' In German, the words 'Come with me' have an ominous ring. They are used when a man is being taken into custody. But there was no getting out of it now, I followed my man away from the platform, nodding to Ted to follow.

We marched through a passageway back to the street. The guide pointed to another entrance and told me to turn to the right. He went back and I continued, loud in my thanks, which were born of relief.

At the ticket window there were more language difficulties. This time an elderly Romanian Saxon jumped into the breach. I got the tickets but found it hard to get rid of my helper. He was curious, but not suspicious. Where did I come from, he wanted to know, and where was I going?

'I'm from the Sudetenland and I'm going down to Bucharest to work for relatives. They've got a job for me there in an iron foundry.'

He said he had asked because my accent was different. I replied as flippantly as I could that I was glad he'd been around, even though it was as hard for me to understand the Saxon dialect as Romanian. He laughed and I moved away to join Ted. I was hot with *Angst*.

'The train doesn't leave until two. Let's get back to the cafes and wait. This place make me nervous.'

We flopped into a coffee shop and raised a cup to the cooperative captain. 'All I can say,' said Ted, 'is that that Jerry was a very decent bloke. And let's hope no one has sent for the cops.'

*

It was time to leave, and we were back on the platform, which was thick with humanity. Soldiers bumped around with kitbags, civilians with packs and suitcases. Children piped and people shouted as the train rolled in, manificent in its cloud of steam, couplings clanking and brakes squealing. On the loud-speaker system a Romanian voice spilled forth incomprehensibly, but we could pick out the words Bucharest, Sofia, Athens.

The black and white boards on the sides of the coaches told the rest of the story: Warsaw, Bratislava, Budapest. This was the transcontinental express and everyone surged forward. We gripped each other by the arm and were swept up the coach steps and into a corridor. The train was already packed but somehow the Brasov crowd got on. There was no hope of getting a seat but for us nothing could have been less important. For the first time in three years we were escaping in style, and almost choked with excitement.

Soon the shouting and pushing died down. Whistles shrilled. The train gave a huge gasp and began to move. It was moving and we were on it and hadn't been caught. Bye-bye, Brasov.

'Watch for the camp,' whispered Ted. 'We'll be passing it.'

The train was going at a fair speed when it clattered by *Lagarul* 14. But the sight of the deserted compounds remains etched in my memory. First we saw the 'hotel'. It was no more than a hundred yards from our fascinated gaze, and there was no sign of any of the officers. Then came the sergeants' compound. Again only guards. Everyone was confined to quarters. Mentally we gave the boys a wave. Physically, we shrank back, afraid that a keen-eyed someone might spot our faces at the coach window. Then we were past, and speeding south.

*

Darkness. Slow progress over the mountains, and several stops. The train is still crowded but at every halt there is an exodus and an influx and we have graduated to the luxury of seats. Once more the shout of brakes and the hiss of steam and now there are calls of '*Ployesht! Ployesht!*' We are in Ploesti, the oil city, and for twenty minutes all is bustle and confusion, because in tribute to the raid of August Ploesti is totally blacked out. In the coaches, dim blue blackout bulbs cast an unreal light over the packed benches.

Off again; I am sitting near the door that leads to the corridor. I cannot see Ted for he is sitting diagonally from me, in the far comer, and half a dozen people are standing between us, hanging on to handstraps. I doze, but not for long. A man is making his way down the passage and even though I understand little Romanian it is easy to make out his mission. He is a railway policeman and is demanding to see papers.

There is a confusion of tumbling thoughts. Should I get up and squeeze farther down the corridor? No. The train is too crowded and Ted is too far away to be able to join me. Besides, movement will attract attention. Sweat it out and hope for the best. Pretend to be asleep.

The man is only three feet away now. 'Papers!' he shouts, and in response the passengers fumble in wallet and handbag. He begins his check on the other side of the carriage and one by one the men and women produce their identity cards. I cannot see Ted but it is clear that he is playing the same game as I am. '*Doarme*,'* says someone as the policeman raises his lantern and peers through the mass. Ted has got away with it. The policeman, who has only one foot in the crowded compartment, is too tired to go over to him. Others hold out the necessary and he is content. But now the man next to me is showing his papers and in seconds it will be my turn. I feel myself being shaken by the shoulder. I give a tiny snore and let my head sag. Incredibly, the policeman gives up, muttering his complaints, and moves away. I keep my eyes closed and snore once more for effect.

*

*'He's asleep.'

The train pulls into Bucharest North at 7.30 pm. Inconspicuous in our shabby civilian suits and overcoats, packs under our arms like a hundred others, we pass the barriers without incident. Outside, this city is also blacked out and there is little traffic on the streets. I leave Ted at a corner and march into one of the many small restaurants that line the area. It is full. *'Telefon?'* The man behind the counter points to a pay phone. I insert a coin and dial the number. No one answers.

Ted is waiting where I had left him. 'We'd better try later. Let's go down the road and find some place where we can disappear for an hour. Wandering streets is bloody dangerous.'

Bucharest seemed to be full of restaurants of all kinds. Music poured into the darkened streets from them and we peered through a dozen doors before choosing one that seemed low-class enough to absorb two untidy beings like us. It was thick with smoke, and waiters ran among the tables with beer and food. A four-man orchestra gave forth with Romanian folk tunes and an occasional piece of German Schmalz. Half a dozen cavorted as the other customers cheered them on. Ted and I slid into an empty seat and when the waiter came up I screamed over the din for beer. He came back with two jugs and gave change. The noise made conversation almost impossible and as we quaffed I thought how crazy it was to be sitting here like this enjoying ourselves in an enemy capital. I winked at Ted and he grinned and sank half his drink at one go. 'Good stuff,' he yelled, but for all anyone heard or cared he might even have been speaking Russian.

The waiter floated up again, an ectoplasm in a white apron. He raised his eyebrows and I lifted two fingers. He dashed off and suddenly I felt elated. There was nothing to this. At this rate we could get to Turkey just by visiting beer halls.

The mood was quickly smashed. Two soldiers had come in at the far end and were making the rounds of the tables. They were military police looking for deserters. I put my drink down and grabbed Ted. But he, too had seen what was happening. We rose as one and made for the door through which we had entered, tugging almost in panic at the covering blackout curtain. Then we were in the street, running through the dark like champions. We stopped two blocks away and listened. There was no chase.

'Come on.'

We returned to the first place and tried to phone again. I felt shaky. Christ, I thought, we are really balling things up, dashing about Bucharest like a couple of idiots. We'll be caught if we go on like this.

A woman's voice broke in, and she asked 'Hello!' twice before I assembled my confused formula.

'Ich bin der schwedische Geschäftsmann. Ich bin eben von Stockholm hergekommen.'

'Just a minute please.'

A man came to the phone. I repeated that I was the Swedish businessman who had just arrived from Stockholm. He asked me what time I got in and I said about seven. He told me to wait. I stood in the cafe with the phone in my hand, scared stiff that the police would appear. The man came on again and asked me where I was.

God help me. I didn't know.

'In a coffee shop near the Bucharest North railway station.'

'Wait at the far corner. The one on the right as you come out of the station entrance. Stand with your feet on the curb and be there at exactly ten o'clock. We'll ask you whether you are from Bofors. *Auf Wiedersehen!*'

'*Auf Wiedersehen!*'

I put the phone down. I had been nervous, and my German had been lousy. Never mind; it had worked. Maybe Swedes spoke lousy German, too.

I gave Ted the good news.

At three minutes to ten we took up position. A car appeared; not ours because it didn't stop. But it looked as if it was going to and it made us jumpy.

Ten o'clock. Several vehicles went by. Maybe they weren't going to pick us up after all. But almost before we were aware of it a black limousine was there and someone was saying something about Bofors. We jumped into the rear seat and were whisked off. We had made our contact. We were saved. Ted poked me in the ribs as the car halted at a main intersection. Like him, I felt exultant.

Two men sat in the front. The one who wasn't driving shook hands with us and asked how it had been in the camp.

'Not too bad.' It was an opinion we felt entitled to. We'd had so much experience. Besides, camps were now a thing of the past.

Our new friends said nothing more and in about twenty minutes the car entered a driveway in a prosperous residential area. The second man jumped out and opened a garage door. The car was driven into the garage and the door closed.

'Wait here,' we were told, and our companions went through a small door into the house.

An hour passes. Two. What can be going on? Was this the way the secret service worked? Not even a cup of coffee for two deserving escapers?

The little door opens again and the two men reappear. They do not look cheerful and their message is sad.

'We're terribly sorry, but the fact is that we can do very little for you right now. There are reasons for this but we can't go into them. You will have to go on your own.'

We gazed at them in disbelief. These men were risking their lives and we had no right to reproach them. But we felt bitter I disappointment. The chances of getting out of the camp and reaching Bucharest had been a hundred to one. And now this.

'What should we do?'

'A train leaves for the Black Sea soon after dawn. Take it. But don't go quite as far as the port. For one thing there'll be security checks just before the train gets in. Second, your best bet isn't Constanta but Medgidia, about twenty miles away. From there you'll be able to strike across the district we call the Dobroja and get into Bulgaria. That's better than trying to get on a ship. The docks are too well guarded. And it should be pretty easy to get down to the border because it's only a few miles from where you get off the train. There are some hills in eastern Bulgaria but no real obstacles, and in a few days you should be in Turkey.'

'Will you buy the tickets for us?'

'You can easily get them yourselves. But we'll coach you in how to ask for them and if anything goes wrong you can always say you're Germans. We'll take you to the station and make sure you get away all right.'

'Are they likely to ask us for papers?'

'No. Not when you buy tickets. Not even in Bucharest. Security checks are only made on trains coming into the capital or approaching ports and frontier points. You should have no difficulty.'

I spent a while learning how to ask in Romanian for two single third-class tickets to Medgidia. Our hosts pronounced themselves satisfied and at dawn we left for the station.

'We'll need a good map.'

'There are plenty at the station. And here is some Bulgarian money. It's more than enough to see you through.'

I pocketed the strange-looking notes and fell silent. The streets had not come to life but at the station all was activity. Hundreds of people sat or slept in the waiting rooms and in the cavernous station hall, and we picked our way through them, followed by our friends. They nodded us towards the correct ticket counter and I brought forth my parrot phrases. The clerk handed over the tickets and said something about which platform to go to. But we knew that already.

The map was bought, the loudspeaker system announced the imminent departure of our train, and we made our way to the barrier. Two policemen were on duty but they said nothing and we passed on to the platform along with everyone else.

I glanced back. Our mysterious companions were watching us, two thick-set figures in dark coats and homburg hats, each about forty years of age. They nodded almost imperceptibly. I returned the salute and, with Ted, boarded the train. Five minutes later it pulled out.

*

The coaches were full at first but by noon, six hours after leaving Bucharest, they were almost empty. There had been only one ticket check and we were feeling confident. No one had tried to speak to us and now we were sitting alone at one end of a coach that had a passage down the centre, much as old-fashioned streetcars used to have. There was a long stop at Lehliu, and we jumped down and bought a pile of food and sprawled on the hard seats, munching away warily but happily as the plain of Wallachia unrolled before us.

'Wonder why those chaps couldn't help?'

'God knows. There was something pretty strange about them. They knew about us otherwise they wouldn't have responded. But they couldn't unload us fast enough. Can't make out why they took the job on in the first place.'

'Maybe they didn't, not really.'

'They must have. Otherwise we wouldn't have been given the telephone number.'

'Well it's clear that they weren't set up properly. If they had been we'd have been taken in and hidden for a few days. As things are we've been spewed forth on our own and for all they know we'll spill the beans. If we're caught, that is. If I'd been them I'd have taken two bodies like us to the frontier and pointed out which way to go.'

'Well, we'll probably never know what was behind it all. But if you ask me they weren't professionals. They were much too nervous, and pros would have bought the tickets in advance. They could easily have gone into the station first and come out with them. Getting us to buy them was just one more risk.'

The train rattled on over the dull countryside, which was totally unlike the parts of Romania with which we were familiar. It was more like the Yorkshire moors, or perhaps the Russian steppes. But in the late afternoon we raised a quiet cheer as we crossed the Danube on the great bridge at Cernavoda. The river had turned north from its long task of forming the Romanian-Bulgarian border, and the change of direction meant it was no longer an obstacle. From now on, Bulgaria was accessible by foot.

There were anti-aircraft guns around the bridge and Ted noted their number.

'Our people in Turkey will want to know that,' he said, 'and look at those marshes. That's the sort of thing you don't see on maps. If we were walking we'd never make it.'

At 4.30 pm the train pulled in at Medgidia. It was a small, unimportant looking place, and once we had bought a few supplies we lost no time in leaving. For escapers, small places are dangerous.

We kept to a dirt road for a mile and then struck south by compass. The frontier, we calculated, was twenty miles away, and the road might be patrolled. We wanted no mistakes, and marched gladly into the oncoming dusk. Sometimes a field worker was to be seen, distant as a figure on a child's painting. But none approached us and soon it was dark.

No moon showed the way and the going got hard.

We stumbled over rocks and holes. Ted hurt his leg, and in the early hours we called a halt.

'Let's wait here until it's light and get the lay of the land. The border can't be any more than eight or nine miles off and we don't want to bump into it by accident.'

It was cold and we shivered and dozed until the day came. The land was bare, with a few ploughed patches. Somehow, we would have to find out where we were. A village – any village – should give us our bearings.

'Let's have something to eat and then move on. We might see something.'

A couple of hours later we breasted a ridge and saw a *melange* of muddy-white houses dominated by a church that looked like a mosque. The sun was up now and its rays glinted from the golden dome.

'Looks all right.'

We struck the road again and marched down the hamlet's single straggling street. Men appeared, dressed in embroidered white shirts and baggy white pants. Suddenly, in our shabby city clothing, we knew we were as conspicuous as tax collectors. But the move had been made and it was too late to draw back. If luck was with us we would get through and disappear before anyone had time to become suspicious.

The important thing was to note the place name on the local administration office, which was opposite the church and set back a little from the road. Early though it was a small crowd clustered there, and anxious not to seem nervous we raised our hands in greeting. The salute was not returned.

We came to the end of the houses and quickened our steps. Behind us someone shouted, and three uniformed men hurried in our direction.

'Let's make a dash for it,' I urged. Ted, whose leg was giving him trouble, shook his head. 'I can't,' he said, and sat down. 'You try. Go on, you might make it.'

There was no time for argument and I ran into a bare field. Five hundred yards away reared a crest covered with uncut corn. I reached it and dived to the ground as a shot whistled past. A dozen men were now advancing in a line, firing and yelling.

I could surrender and perhaps be hit as I stood to signal or I could break for the terrain beyond the cover and run a gauntlet of bullets. But I had neither the strength nor the courage to do either so I hugged the earth, hoping that the pursuit might miss me.

There was no chance. A bullet ripped through the corn not a yard away. Then the shooting stopped and two minutes later a peasant policeman was pointing his weapon at my head. I raised my arms and tried to stand up, but fatigue and the emotion of failure were too much. My knees gave way and I sat down, comically, hands still in the air.

*

Collins and Lancaster were finally liberated by the Russians on Romania's collapse in 1944 and flown to England in an American bomber. Both men were awarded the Military Medal. Today, Collins lives in Vancouver and works as a television journalist for the Canadian Broadcasting Corporation.

Wing-Commander E. Garrad-Cole was the pilot of a Blenheim bomber, shot down over Tobruk on 15 July 1940. He spent the next three and a half years in Italian prison camps. Then came the Italian surrender – and the grim prospect of all Allied PoWs in the country being sent to camps in the heart of Germany. It was then that Garrad-Cole made his last desperate attempt for freedom – an attempt that was to lead him to the steps of St Peter's in Rome . . .

8

Single to Rome

For bedding, there was a layer of dung and straw. A tin can stood in one corner to serve as a toilet.

Twenty-five of us, all British prisoners of war, were locked in the last truck of a cattle train, groaning slowly along the Italian track towards Rome. After three and a half years in Italian hands we were being moved for a further spell in Germany – and the thought was unendurable. Fane Harvey and I decided to escape at all costs.

In the prison camp at Frosinone, about seventy miles southeast of Rome, we had managed to steal an axe, which Fane had tucked down the leg of the baggy trousers he was wearing, and we quickly made a thorough inspection of our surroundings. The floor was too thick for us to hack a way through, and if we made a hole in either side or in the roof, almost certainly we should be seen leaving. The only hope seemed to be to chop a hole in the boards at the end of the truck, so we hacked away carefully without severing the wood on the outside of the truck, At the right moment we would kick away the rectangle of timber we had weakened.

While we were discussing our plans, the train ground to a halt. Suddenly there was a hum of excited conversation from the guards outside our truck. Had they spotted something? Splinters perhaps? We did not know. Now, for the first time, the doors were being unlocked. A German entered with a torch and pushed his way between us straight to the far end of the truck where we had been at work.

We had plastered the chopped boards with dung, but the camouflage did not seem very effective to us. We waited, hardly breathing. The guard flashed his torch over the walls, muttered something unintelligible in German and then departed. The doors were bolted and the train moved on. We breathed again.

We dared not wait any longer. As we felt the momentum gathering, we kicked out the boards and clambered through the hole on to the buffers. An icy blast struck at us. We seemed to be going too fast for our purpose and we hung on as long as we could. Then, when our hands were almost completely numbed and we knew we would fall off if we didn't act at once, we jumped. Fane Harvey went first and was immediately swallowed up by the darkness. Clenching my teeth and shutting my eyes, I leapt. A terrifying moment of hurtling through space. A crash that seemed to have broken every bone in my body. And I was rolling down an embankment.

We guessed that as soon as our escape was discovered, the Germans would concentrate their search along the track. So we struck off into the fields, heading east. We had no money and no food. As to our whereabouts, we only knew we could not be far from Rome.

For about thirty minutes we walked, scarcely speaking. My hands and knees were badly lacerated by the flints at the side of the track, but Fane, apart from being a little shaken, was in reasonable shape.

Cautiously we approached a light in the distance. It came from a small hut, obviously a shepherd's shelter. Sheep were flocking round it but, fortunately for us, there was no sign of a dog to raise the alarm. We made a quick recce and decided on a bold approach.

We walked up to the doorway and flung aside the sacking that served as a door. To our relief we saw there was only one person there: an old man crouched over a small charcoal brazier. He didn't start, didn't even seem surprised. He just turned his head slowly and looked at us steadily.

For a moment we just stared back at him. Then we explained, in halting Italian that we were British PoWs who had escaped from a German prison train. He nodded slowly in understanding and, I thought, smiled very faintly.

After he had given us warm water to clean our wounds, he told us that we were not far from Orte. This was good news to Fane who had been this way before on an earlier escape bid and had stayed with some friendly Italians. We decided that our best plan was to try to find them again. We thanked the old man for his kindness and set out again into the night . . .

*

'Walk boldly up to the booking-office window and say "Single to Rome".' It was the morning of the fifth day after Fane and I had made our leap for freedom, and his Italian friend was coaching us on the next stage of our escape. 'Hand over the exact fare and do not speak to anyone aboard the train. At the other end German soldiers may be checking identity cards, but they will only check a few. Watch your chance and pass through the barrier one by one. Good luck.'

With a firm handshake and a wave, our guide slipped away into the half-light of dawn, leaving us alone in our borrowed clothes, with the money and the map of Rome he had given us.

There was no difficulty about the tickets. The booking-clerk handed them over without so much as a glance at us. The train, when it arrived, was very crowded and we stood wedged firmly amongst civilians, some

Italians in uniform and several German soldiers. I didn't want to meet anyone's gaze, and thus perhaps inadvertently invite conversation, so I pretended to doze.

At our destination we slipped quickly into the midst of the crowd surging towards the ticket barrier. I went on ahead of Fane and then hung back until a man was selected by the German soldiers for inspection.

This was it. Gambling on the theory that they would not pick on two persons in quick succession, I strode along, trying to look casual about it, but feeling tense and slightly sick.

I thrust my ticket into an outstretched hand and kept right on walking. Within a few moments Fane was at my elbow. We didn't look at one another or speak. Soon we were out in the streets of Rome. After three bitter years in captivity and the disappointment of numerous unsuccessful escapes, it was like a dream. The streets crowded with people, the shops, the cars, the pretty girls muffled against the chill early December wind – I couldn't believe I was really there at all, that this really was me walking through an enemy-occupied city.

Our recollection of the street plan we had studied was perfect. As boldly as we could we strode on into the weak sunshine slanting across the Piazza del Popolo, on to the banks of the Tiber. We were heading for St Peter's, partly because we happened to know what it looked like and partly because we thought we would be most likely thereabouts to find someone to whom we might speak without risk of being denounced – a priest, perhaps.

At length we came upon its great mass, dominating the skyline of Rome, with the neutral Vatican City behind it. We knew that a great many Allied subjects had taken refuge in the Vatican City, but we had no thought of entering it. Even supposing we could get past the guards, and this was extremely improbable, we could not hope to get out again before the end of the war. We wanted to get back to our units – Fane to his tanks and I to a squadron.

So now we climbed the wide steps of St Peter's and, at the top, stopped for the first time to look about us. My heart was pounding uncontrollably. I looked at Fane; his face seemed very pale and drawn.

We had arrived, but what now?

We watched the German soldiers on the other side of the square. We watched the civilians and wondered which were enemy agents; which were keeping watch on the Vatican; which might be watching us. We could not help thinking what might happen if we were challenged. A bullet, perhaps . . . if we were lucky.

We looked towards the entrance to the Vatican, where the Swiss guards in their picturesque uniforms stood stolidly on watch. We looked towards the entrance to the cathedral and saw many people entering and leaving. After a quick discussion we decided to approach the first benevolent-looking priest we saw. Picking one out, we walked up to him, and Fane, in his best Italian said: 'We are British prisoners of war,' Just like that.

The priest stopped in his tracks. His jaw dropped in amazement. He looked quickly around, but for a moment he did not reply.

Then, gathering his wits, he muttered: 'I cannot help you . . . but wait here for half an hour . . . I will bring someone who speaks English.' With that he went scampering away as fast as he could go without breaking into a trot.

Had he really gone to fetch help – or to telephone to the Germans or Fascists? We couldn't tell. We could only wait.

*

When I set off for a dawn raid from El Daba on 15 July 1940, little did I think that it would eventually lead me to the steps of St Peter's.

We were shot down near Tobruk after attacking an enemy concentration at El Gazala. Our short-nosed Blenheim hit the sand in a cloud of dust which immediately gave the impression that the aircraft was on fire. I scrambled up in my seat, undoing my straps and parachute harness, shouting at the same time to my navigator to get out. Then, realizing that he had been hit and could not move, I undid his straps and clambered out through the roof, pulling him after me. Then the Italians surrounded us, and for the time being my war was over.

The incidents flashed through my mind as Fane and I waited for the priest to return. Was it really freedom beckoning us now? Or just another recapture, an ignominious return to the hell we had known before? After all we had been through . . .

My first escape was from the camp at Sulmona, in Italy, whence we had been taken from North Africa. With David Pike, an old friend of mine in the RAF and Lieutenant Pope from the Navy, we managed to steal some Italian uniforms, which we hid carefully awaiting a favourable opportunity. During the afternoon of 21 January, 1941, we noticed that one of the sentries was not on duty and that one could scale the corner wall without being seen by either of the other two sentries to north and south.

Quickly changing into our Italian uniforms, we made preparations for our departure. David would go over first and place against the wall a small ladder that we had made. Pope and myself were to follow and use David's ladder to get over the wire. Assistants inside the wire would haul the ladder back after us. Then we would stroll away from the camp trying to look like Italian soldiers going off duty.

Everything went according to plan and we were

soon standing on the far side of the wire and walking slowly up the hill. By this time the sentry was back at his post and gave us a cheerful wave. We waved back.

The going was rough, but by midnight we were clear of our valley and had reached the snow-line on the range of hills running to the south-east. Our original plan was to walk to an Italian air-field at Foggia, some 100 miles to the south of Sulmona, where we hoped to steal an aircraft and fly to Malta, but we abandoned this scheme after a day and a night facing the blizzard.

The weather was against us and we could not hope to reach Foggia before our food ran out. Instead, we would make for the Adriatic coast, with the hope of stealing a boat and sailing to Yugoslavia or Greece.

On the seventh night we reached the coast near the mouth of the Sangro river. We lay motionless in the sand watching for any signs of movement among the boats which had been drawn up clear of the water.

About thirty yards up the beach we could see a wooden hut, the sort of place one would expect fishermen to use for storing their tackle. It seemed to be an ideal place from which to continue our observation. Slowly we got up and walked towards it. We were within a few yards of it when the door opened. An armed Italian shouted: 'Halt!'

We tried to bluff him that we were Italian soldiers

on leave, but it was no use. Two days later we were behind bars in the fortress of Aquila, beginning thirty days' solitary confinement. . .

*

Those thirty days seemed as nothing compared with the thirty minutes we had to wait on the steps of St Peter's. Could our nerves stand it? Could we remain unnoticed and unchallenged all that time? The minutes dragged by. Those two chaps down there in the roadway – weren't they the same two who had passed that way just now?

Fifteen minutes gone. A party of German soldiers marching towards us in the distance, out in Rome itself. Ah, they have turned off to the right.

Twenty, twenty-five minutes. A car draws up with a screech of tyres. Four men come hurrying up the steps towards us. Two pass on one side of us, two on the other. And they keep on going.

Thirty minutes gone. And no sign of our priest or of 'someone' who speaks English. Should we risk waiting any longer? Yes – give him another ten minutes . . .

I began to think of that other occasion in September 1943, when freedom seemed just around the corner. There had been other desperate attempts to break out in the meantime, of course but all proved abortive. Then came the day when our Senior British Officer told us: 'Gentlemen, the Commandant has just informed me that the Italian Government has declared an Armistice.'

Italy was out of the war! This was the moment we had been waiting for! Would the Commandant hand us over to the Germans? Or hand over the camp to us? Or would we have to take control by force?

The Commandant agreed to hand over the camp, but suggested we all remained where we were until further instructions were received from Rome. Our SBO agreed to this on condition that we might take the necessary precautions against any surprise seizure by the Germans. That evening we cut gaps in the barbed wire defences so that we could disperse quickly if any Germans appeared.

Just after lunch on the second day after the Armistice a column of German vehicles were seen moving towards the camp. As soon as he heard this the SBO gave the order to disperse. 'It's every man for himself,' he said.

With three others, I made for the hilly country to the south of the camp, near the village of Rivergaro where we contacted some friendly farmers. Listening to the news bulletin on their radio we soon realized that the Germans were not going to withdraw from Italy and that the Allies would have to fight for every inch of Italian soil.

After about ten days we became very restless. The Allies had landed at Salerno, but there was no news of any landings farther north. We felt that we could not presume any longer on the hospitality of this small community of poor but extremely generous peasants. We decided to strike out south and somehow try to get through to the Allied lines.

By the time we reached Villalgo, to the south-west of Sulmona, it was nearing the end of October and winter was fast approaching. We had not been long in the village before we were told that there were some British parachutists resting in a barn on the outskirts of the village. Our informant agreed to take us to them.

As we opened the door of their hideout we found ourselves looking down the barrel of a machine-carbine. At first we thought this was a trap and that the parachutists were Germans and not English. But we were soon put at ease by a Cockney voice from the darkness asking us how we were. When once we had established that we were bona fide PoWs, we were invited inside to join in their meal.

At first, naturally enough, we thought we had stumbled upon some of the parachutists who, so we had heard, were being dropped to help escaped PoWs. But the captain in charge disillusioned us. They were there to carry out acts of sabotage against the German lines of communication. However, they were able to give us useful information, a map and some money with which to buy rations for the last stage of our journey.

The weather became progressively colder as we went. On the second day after leaving the parachutists we were on the slopes of a 7,000 foot mountain called La Meta. As darkness fell, the wind began to get up and the snow started to fall. Within ten minutes we were battling our way into the teeth of a raging blizzard. It was bitterly cold and we were not clad for this type of weather. Before long our hands and feet became numb with cold and we were staggering along in an exhausted condition. We had been without rest for thirty-six hours.

Somehow, we found our way up the mountain-side, pitching forward every so often to lie in the snow while we regained sufficient strength to carry on. But in the early hours of the morning we had to give up. We came thankfully upon a deserted woodman's hut and sank down on its earthen floor trying to regain our strength.

I had only been asleep for a short while before I was awakened by the sound of German voices outside the hut. We lay there petrified, not daring to move. The door burst open and a torch flashed inside the hut.

An exclamation in German, which I didn't understand, was followed by the sound of a rifle bolt being shot home. We all scrambled to our feet as two German soldiers stepped inside and waved us against the far wall. After two months of freedom we were prisoners again.

At a large Italian barracks at Frosinone, now taken over by the Germans, we began our third imprisonment. Then one night we learned that we were to leave by train the following morning for Germany – on the journey which was to end in Fane and I becoming fugitives in Rome . . .

*

Then more minutes had gone by. And now at last we noticed a fresh-complexioned young priest walking towards us. Yes, he was going to speak to us.

'So you are British prisoners,' he said, in excellent English. 'I think I know of someone who might be prepared to hide you for a time. I will go off and contact him. I might be gone some little time, but don't worry – I'll try to be back within an hour.'

After about forty-five agonizing minutes we saw him coming towards us with a stoutish, middle-aged civilian. Just before they reached us they changed direction slightly and entered the cathedral. This mystified us and we were forced to wait yet another five minutes before the priest emerged. This time he was alone.

Quietly he told us that the Italian, with whom he had entered the cathedral, had agreed to shelter us for a time until other arrangements could be made.

'When he comes out of St Peter's,' the priest said, 'follow him, keeping about ten yards behind. He will lead you to a tram stop, where you will stand next to him, but on no account must you let it appear that you are in company with him. When he boards the tram, you follow and sit where you can see him. Don't bother about tickets. He will buy them for you. The tram ride will take about ten minutes. Follow him again when he gets off, keeping well behind.' With an encouraging smile he said, 'Good luck,' and walked away across the piazza.

Once more we were alone, as we stood on the steps of St Peter's in Rome, and waited for our mysterious guide.

*

We waited for nearly ten minutes before our guide appeared. Then we followed him at a safe distance across the piazza to a nearby tram stop. A tram came up and halted. One or two people got on to it, but our guide remained where he was. After a further short while, a second tram arrived and we clambered aboard on the heels of our guide.

The tram was full, but Fane and I squeezed ourselves into a space on one of the hard wooden seats where we could keep our guide under observation. Our tickets had been paid for us as we had entered the tram so that we now had nothing to do until we reached our destination.

Ten minutes passed before our guide got up from his seat, ready to alight at the next stop. We waited until the tram halted then got up and followed him out into the street, hurrying around comers until finally we saw our guide pass through a gateway in a high brick wall. We followed him inside and he bolted the door behind us. Then he turned and, in good English, said, 'This is the British Embassy garden!'

It appeared that our guide, whose name was Secundo, had in peacetime been employed as caretaker. Now the Embassy was locked and deserted, except for the few rooms Secundo occupied with his family on the first floor. 'I shall be delighted if you will stay with me until something more suitable can be arranged,' he said.

We stayed with Secundo for several days, keeping well inside the building during the day, taking our exercise in the garden at night. We slept luxuriously in large single beds which must once have been used by Embassy secretaries, and consumed quantities of fine champagne which we managed to filch from the Embassy cellars. But after a time Secundo became anxious. He felt sure he was being followed and that the Germans were suspicious. We had to leave straight away.

The priest who had arranged our hideout was contacted again, and he took Fane and me first to a Lithuanian seminary, where we spent a miserable ten days, and then to an Italian family who were already sheltering some British prisoners of war.

Our new hosts were Renzo Luccidi and his wife Adrienne, and we were soon introduced to the three young men they were harbouring – Jock Simpson, John Firman and Pat Wilson. The flat was not overlarge and there was room for only one more. So it was arranged that Fane should remain there and that I should go along with Pat Wilson to a French seminary where he was living with several other PoWs. It was a few days before Christmas 1943, and as I walked along the crowded streets with Pat I could sense an air of gaiety in spite of the privations the German occupation had brought.

We spent a quiet Christmas in the seminary (I remember listening to the King's speech on the wireless which gave me a great thrill and made me long to be back in England), and afterwards began to move about Rome much more freely, either singly or in pairs. Our days were spent either in helping Luccidi to distribute food to prisoners in hiding, and for whom he was caring, or else in searching for information which might be of use to the Allies.

We had to be careful, though. In the daytime the Germans were in the habit of suddenly cordoning off a street, after which they would examine the identity cards of everyone caught in their trap. Any Italians they found of military age were taken away for deportation to Germany or sent to work in labour battalions in the north, where the Germans were still building defensive positions in the mountains. Luccidi had arranged forged identity cards for us. But they would not be of much use if we were going to be deported.

It was not long after this that we heard on the radio that the Allies had landed at Anzio, and this raised our morale tremendously. It used to give me an enormous kick, also, to watch the waves of American Flying Fortresses come over. Occasionally we saw an aerial battle between the escorting Spitfires and any German FX 190s that dared to try to interfere with the bombers. On one occasion the sirens went as I was delivering some food to a party of other ranks who were living with an Italian widow and her family on the outskirts of the city. A railway line ran close by the house, and before we knew what was happening, bombs were falling within 100 yards of us. The widow and her children were petrified, but we managed to pacify them between us and the raid was soon over.

*

I went outside shortly afterwards to see what damage had been done. No sooner had I turned the corner at the top of the road than I realized that something was wrong. I could see a party of Germans herding Italian civilians into several lorries that were parked across the street.

Hastily I turned to go in the opposite direction, but I had not gone far before I saw another party of Germans cordoning off the road ahead of me. I had stumbled into a trap and had to act quickly.

Fortunately there were quite a number of people about and this gave me a chance to search for an alleyway. Turning down the first one I saw, I came up against a high brick wall. There was a door in the wall, but when I tried the handle, I found it to be bolted on the other side.

Suddenly I heard footsteps behind me. I turned expecting to see a German with a gun pointing at me. Instead I saw a panic-stricken Italian looking for a way out of the trap. Quickly I made him let me climb on his shoulders until I could reach the top of the wall and haul myself up. Once on the top I leaned over and grasped the Italian's outstretched hand and pulled him up after me. We dropped down the other side together, to find ourselves at the back of a house, in a courtyard which led into an adjoining street.

After making quite certain that the street was clear I shook hands with the Italian and set off home as fast as my legs would carry me. I learned afterwards that an air-raid shelter had been hit during the bombing, killing 150 people, and that the Germans had only been rounding up a working party to clear up the mess.

During the first week in February I went into the Vatican for the first time. In the Italian prison camp at Sulmona I had met an Irish priest named Monsignore O'Flaherty who accompanied the Pope's representative on visits to the camp. I knew now that he was helping to shelter Allied prisoners in Rome and I sent a message to him. In reply came an invitation to take tea with him in the Vatican.

On arriving at the main gate I was halted by the picturesque Swiss guards. I produced my identity card and told them in my best Italian that I had come to see Monsignore O'Flaherty. When I was ushered to the priest's apartment, I was astonished to find several of my friends, whom I had first met at the Luccidis' flat, and we had an amusing tea party.

It had become necessary to change our hideout, and we explained the predicament to O'Flaherty. 'I think I can help you,' he said, shaking my hand. 'I'll let you know in a day or two.'

The following day I received a message from Monsignore O'Flaherty for myself and a friend, Gill, to go to an address in the Via Pariolo at six o'clock that evening. We would find somebody there who had agreed to look after us.

*

Punctually at six o'clock Gill and I knocked on the door of a rather attractive Roman villa in the fashionable quarter. The door was opened by a middle-aged maid who immediately beckoned us inside without speaking and ushered us into a beautifully furnished room.

As we entered, a tall, attractive blonde with blue-grey eyes got up from a settee and came across the room to greet us. I will call her Christina (that is not her real name). She was a *marchesa* and came from the north of Italy, but also kept an apartment in Rome. She spoke several languages, including English, almost perfectly. And, having spent much time in Britain before the war, was passionately fond of all things English. For the Nazis and Fascists she had nothing but contempt and bitter hatred.

Christina explained that the flat we were in belonged to a friend of hers, who was no longer in Rome. She slept there at night in case the Germans should look for her at her own address. She was mixed up in a number of anti-Fascist and anti-German organizations and, although she did not think the Germans knew of her activities, she considered it prudent to play safe.

During the rest of my stay in the Italian capital Christina was to be my almost constant guide and companion. In her company I was able to move about Rome almost as freely as any Roman; she insisted on taking me to a high-class tailor where I had a suit made for me; and we ate in fashionable restaurants. The war for me had taken a bizarre turn that was at times almost incredible.

Christina and I were returning to the flat one day in a crowded tram, having just finished an excellent lunch at 'The Bear', when I noticed two German SS soldiers standing next to us. At first I paid no attention to them, but after a time I began to realize that they were taking much too much interest in me. At once I decided to get off at the next stop. If they followed, it would confirm my suspicions and at the same time draw them away from Christina.

With a whispered explanation, I pushed my way out of the tram and started to saunter down a side street.

I glanced anxiously over my shoulder. The Germans had also left the tram and were following – about twenty yards behind me. I had to think fast. This was the biggest threat to my liberty since I had arrived in Rome.

Frantically I tried to form a plan of escape. When I had left the tram I had not noticed where we were, but now, I realized I was at the Porta del Popolo, not far from the Luccidis.

Now I tried to convince myself that perhaps it was merely a coincidence that the Germans had left the tram at that point. I stopped to look in a shop window, to see what they would do. Holding my breath I watched their reflections in the window as they passed behind me. They walked straight on, not even glancing in my direction, and I sighed with relief.

But then they stopped about twenty yards away, to look in another shop window. My heart sank. Obviously the Huns were playing me at my own game. With every intention of arresting me, they were stringing me along, perhaps in the hope that I might lead them to something or someone bigger – to someone like Luccidi for instance.

I began to walk back the way I had come and turned sharp right down a side street. As soon as I was round the corner I began to quicken my pace. But already I could hear the pounding of German jack-boots and it was only a matter of seconds before they came up one on either side of me.

'*Carta d'identicita*,' said one of them with a strong German accent.

Without speaking I produced my forged identity card and handed it to him. He scrutinized it carefully and then showed it to his chum.

Shaking his index finger at me he said: '*Nix est buono!*' I tried to bluff. It was no use. The two of them, still one on either side of me, pushed me forward and marched me up the street.

As I went along I thought of the grim tales I had heard of the brutality and torture to which prisoners of the SS were subjected. My only hope seemed to be to act quickly; to make quite certain that I got away with the least possible delay.

We were walking towards the Piazza del Popolo as I glanced at my escorts, endeavouring to weigh up my chances. They were armed only with pistols, which they carried in holsters at their waists. They were shorter than myself but quite hefty. I decided to chance it.

Suddenly I stuck out my right leg, tripping my right-hand escort so that he staggered forward. As he staggered, I struck him behind the ear with all my might. He fell to the ground. I stepped quickly forward and rushed down the street. A moment later I heard a bullet whine past my shoulder and saw it strike the wall of a house a few yards ahead of me. Several more bullets followed but they seemed to be well off target. By this time women passers-by were screaming and everybody was rushing to take cover. In a way this was a good thing. It enabled me to race along unimpeded by pedestrians.

Luckily I was quite close to Luccidi's flat and, realizing that my only hope was to get off the streets before I ran headlong into some more Germans, I decided to make for it. I was definitely drawing away from my pursuers, probably because they were hampered by their heavy jack-boots.

Running for my life now, I rounded the corner of the block in which the Luccidis were living. I paused at the entrance to glance over my shoulder – there was no one in sight. I dived into the doorway and hid myself behind a pillar in the hall. Within seconds I heard the pounding of jack-boots on the pavement outside and caught a glimpse of my pursuers as they flashed past the entrance. I rushed up the stairs to the fifth floor and, gasping for breath, pounded on the door of the Luccidis' flat.

As quickly and coherently as I could, I told Renzo what had happened. 'Go up and hide on the roof,' he said. 'They will search the block as soon as they realize you have given them the slip.'

I bounded up two more flights to the flat roof. Then I spotted a small wooden hut which housed the machinery for the lift.

'Go and bring the lift to the top floor,' I shouted. And without question Renzo obeyed.

I waited on the top landing for the lift to come up. Then with some difficulty I climbed on the top of the cage to lie full length in the small space between the top of the cage and the winding gear.

'Try and put the lift out of order,' I whispered to Renzo. Then, as he disappeared down the stairs, I lay there, soaked in perspiration, panting for air yet hardly daring to breathe.

Suddenly, there was an outburst of shouting, followed by the sound of many heavy footsteps. The search had started. For nearly an hour, I lay there as the Germans went from one flat to another, pushing their way in to check up on the occupants. Gradually they came closer as they worked their way up the stairs. I prayed hard that the lift was out of order. If it was not, I might at any moment find myself descending into full view of the Germans.

I heard steps on the top flight of stairs. They passed through the door and on to the roof. They were only gone a couple of minutes before they came back and went clattering down the stairs. Gradually the sounds of the hunt faded into the distance as the search party withdrew.

A few minutes later I came out of my hiding place and discussed with Renzo the best way of getting out of the building. He insisted that I must go without delay, for the Germans would be sure to come back and search more thoroughly. In the end it was decided that I should change my overcoat and hat, in case my description had been circulated, and go out with Renzo's small son, Maurice, holding my hand.

Together little Maurice and I walked out of the building and turned left towards the Tiber. I could see knots of watchful Germans standing on the street corners ahead of us. As we approached the first corner my heart began to thump, but Maurice kept up a steady chatter and we went by without more than a glance from the Germans. We had to pass two more groups before we reached at last the banks of the Tiber and comparative safety. Here Maurice said *au revoir* and, with a cheerful wave, went scampering off home. I went to some friends of Christina's, a couple who lived just off the Piazza Venezia, who agreed to take me in.

Christina arrived after lunch the next day, looking attractive, smart, cool and unconcerned. She did not give any indication of the anxiety she must have experienced after I had left her on the tram. Yet, if I had been caught and the fact that she had been helping me had been discovered, she could not have expected any mercy from the Germans.

The SS now had my identity card, which contained my photograph. It was unlikely that this would be circulated for at least a day, so I was reasonably certain of not being recognized at the moment, but obviously I would have to change my appearance as soon as possible. During the next fortnight, while I remained hidden at the flat, I began growing a moustache, trained my hair differently, assumed a bow tie and began to wear horn-rimmed spectacles. Then Christina made arrangements for me to be photographed again and a new identity card was prepared. I was all set to go back into circulation.

A few weeks later we heard on the radio that the Allies had launched a major offensive against the Gustav line. This was terrific news and from that day on we listened in to almost every news bulletin from London, eagerly crossing off on a map in front of us the place-names as they fell to the Allies.

In the city itself there was an air of tense excitement, but outwardly everybody remained calm. The Germans must have realized that their days in the city were numbered because they renewed their efforts to round up as many people as possible. Time and again they threw cordons across the streets.

In these circumstances it became more and more dangerous to move about and most of us refrained from going out unless it was really necessary. On 4 June we heard that Marshal Kesselring, asking the Pope to convey to the Allies his proposal that Rome should be considered an open city, had undertaken to evacuate his troops from the city and to refrain from carrying out any demolitions within the city limits. The Allies were in the outskirts of Rome that morning and the German rearguard put up their final resistance before pulling out.

*

As soon as things had quietened down, Christina and I went out together, armed with a bottle of wine to search for some of our friends to welcome the Allies into the city. American infantry had taken up positions round the Piazza and I found an American colonel with a wireless jeep alongside the beautiful fountain in the centre.

I thought it my duty to report my presence in the city to the Allies as soon as possible, so I went up to the colonel and said:

'I am a Royal Air Force officer and I have been living in Rome for the last six months.'

'You don't say! I'm sure glad to meet you,' he said, stretching out his hand.

'And I'm certainly glad to see you,' I said, shaking his outstretched hand.

By this time the whole of the population of Rome seemed to be out to cheer the Allies. The girls were climbing on stationary tanks to embrace the tank crews and ply them with wine. British, Italian and American flags were everywhere and every vehicle that passed down the street was pelted with roses. Everybody was out – really enjoying life for the first time since the

German occupation, or perhaps since the beginning of the war.

We went back to the flat and danced to gramophone records until just before dawn. I could still hear the rumble of tanks and the cheering of the crowds as I fell into a very deep and peaceful sleep.

To be captured by the Japanese was the nightmare that haunted every Allied airman who flew in the Far East during the Second World War, for capture by the Japanese Army often meant summary execution. Fears were intensified by propaganda pictures, showing British and American aircrews being beheaded.

When Flight Sergeant Cyril Copley and his Liberator crew were shot down over Thailand, it was this kind of fear that drove them on to avoid capture at all costs. Capture would have meant torture, too, for their squadron was a 'special duties' unit whose task was to drop agents and supplies to resistance movements in South-East Asia.

As it turned out, the Japanese were not the only ones interested in the fate of the Liberator crew – who, unwittingly, had crash-landed right in the middle of a Secret Service intrigue designed to set the whole of Thailand aflame.

9

Fugitives in Siam
'Two fighters over on the starboard, skipper.'

Fair-haired Flight Sergeant Cyril ('Curly') Copley, P for Peter's twenty-three-year-old Yorkshire rear gunner, stiffened at the bomb-aimer's sudden warning over the intercom. He tightened his grip on the triggers of his two.5s as he sat hunched in the rear turret of his No 358 Squadron Liberator at half-past six on the morning of 29 May 1945. The Liberator, on a top-secret mission from its base at Jessore, Calcutta, was within half an hour of dropping three American officers to join Thai underground forces deep in the interior of Jap-occupied Thailand (Siam). As he peered out of the turret, straining his eyes in search of the hostile fighters, he noticed that there was not a scrap of cloud within reach into which they could nip to seek refuge. And then, scanning the sunlit sky 6,000 feet above the dense green jungle,

Copley saw two more fighters. Altogether, there were nine Japs and they were formatting in three vies directly ahead of the Liberator. Curly tensed as the voice of his Canadian skipper, Flying Officer Harry ('Smithy') Smith crackled in the ear-phones: 'Watch them, gunners. They're turning in to attack.' The Liberator jinked from side to side as Smithy weaved to avoid the impending head-on onslaught.

Suddenly, Copley heard a colossal clanging noise behind him like hail rattling on a tin roof. Jap cannon-shells were ripping into the top of the Lib's fuselage as the first enemy fighter made its attack. The acrid smell of burning cordite filled Curly's nostrils. As the Jap broke away down to port, Copley glimpsed the dirty-brown fighter as clearly as in a recognition book. An Oscar! Swivelling his turret, he checked range and deflection.

A second later, another Oscar flashed past. The Liberator juddered awkwardly as the second-pilot, hit head-on by a cannon-shell, slumped across his control column, making the aircraft difficult to control. The navigator, too, was soon shot-up. Copley swung his turret and squirted with his guns as Jap after Jap disappeared far below.

A few seconds afterwards, in a flash, Copley saw the elevator trimming-tab just beside him fly off and go floating down. This shook him for he realized how close the enemy shells were coming. But still he bore a charmed life, for none hit him.

Out of the corner of his eye, Copley saw white smoke pouring back. He heard the engines spluttering and knew they were hit and on fire. Steadily, in attack after merciless attack, the nine Oscars hit one after another of the Liberator's engines until, finally, all four were practically out of action. The plane was losing height rapidly.

Fortunately, the intercom, which had been transmitting only scraps of noise for some minutes, now had a spasm of life. And then Copley heard the shattering message from the skipper:

'Prepare for crash-landing.'

Unplugging his intercom, he climbed out of his turret and scrambled down into his crash-landing station, beside the waist-gun positions. Here he found an absolute melee of six struggling bodies. Some of them had not been on intercom and so had failed to hear the crash-landing message. Several were clipping on 'chutes, or already had them in position on their chests. They had the rear escape-hatch open and were preparing to jump. As Copley glanced out of the hatch he saw the solid green of the jungle only a few hundred feet below. 'We're crash-landing,' he screamed madly, to stop those about to jump from committing certain suicide.

The seven men had hardly got into their crash-landing positions on the floor when they felt the first terrific crash, and heard a crunching rending of metal as the Liberator hit the tree-tops. Immediately afterwards, a second colossal jolt followed as the kite tore through the trees and ploughed along the deck. Flung back by the impact, Copley blacked out.

*

When he came round, a few seconds later, he found himself in a large detached section of the fuselage. The smell of burning fuel and dope was overwhelming. Gazing dazedly round, he suddenly saw that his section was blazing. He prepared to get out quickly. But, pulling himself up, he discovered that one of his feet was trapped. The flames were licking nearer. He wrenched his leg hard and the foot came out, leaving the shoe wedged in the fuselage. He pushed his way through a gap in the wreckage and limped out.

Standing among the jungle shrubs, he stared at chunks of wreckage scattered in all directions. Orange flames and black smoke spiralled up from the blazing metal. Mingling with the oily fumes was the nauseating smell of bodies burning. Surely, Copley thought, no one else could have got out alive.

A wave of anger flooded through Curly's mind as he stood there, alone. This had been the final op of his tour. He had at last got the boat in sight after four years overseas. Yet, now, here he was down in the middle of the Thai jungle, about a thousand miles from the nearest Allied territory with more than 100,000 Japanese troops around him in a country that was at war with the Allies – and there appeared to be no hope whatever of getting back. What was worse, he seemed to be the only survivor. This would have to happen to him!

Just as he was thinking 'Poor old Smithy', to his astonishment his skipper walked round the front portion of the crackling kite. Flying Officer Smith looked as grey as ash. Blood was streaming down his face from a ghastly gash in his scalp which hung limply down in a jagged four-inch flap. But he was alive. Curly heaved an enormous sigh of relief that he had not been left on his own in these alien surroundings.

With rounds of ammunition exploding in every direction, Copley and Smith dragged the others out of the kite. Then one of the Wops, Flight Sergeant Ray (Timber) Woods, appeared round the far side of the burning fuselage. Blood dripped down his face and he could hardly speak because of a piece of shrapnel blocking his nose. With him came the other Wop, Flight Sergeant Bill (Whacker) Pugh. A bullet through the centre of one of his hands had made the hand useless.

Having rescued everyone it was possible to get out, Curly Copley took stock of the state of the crew. The navigator, Flight Sergeant 'Lofty' Brenchley, was lying fifteen to twenty yards from the aircraft, lifeless. The second pilot, Flight Sergeant Bob Poole, was dead in the cockpit. The mid-upper gunner, Flight Sergeant Bill Pinkney, was in the telescoped crackling front section. Bomb-aimer Flight Sergeant Jack Draper was trapped in the bomb-bay, where he had been crushed to death when the kite had hit. The dispatcher, Flight Sergeant Bill ('Taffy') Parsons, had a bullet through one foot.

Of the Americans, Major Johnny Gildee had a broken shoulder, while Lieutenant Reid S. Moore, who had come along to witness the other three Americans jump, was so seriously burned that he could hardly move. The remaining two Americans were in an even more sorry state. Sergeant E. J. ('Mac') MacCarthy was badly shot up and his back was broken. Worst of all was Corporal 'Nap' Naparolski, who had a gaping hole in his stomach. He was moaning horribly and every movement was agony. While Curly Copley ached and had a few scratches along his back, he and Flight Sergeant Ramsey Roe, the screen dispatcher, were the only persons who had not got some kind of serious injury. In all, ten of the original fourteen in the crew had survived.

Holding a quick conference, the shot-down airmen decided they had got to leave the prang as quickly as possible. The attacking Oscars would report their position and the Japanese patrol would undoubtedly be sent out to search for them. They determined to set off for the hills. There, they would stand less chance of coming across a Jap camp and they might be able to join up with Free Thai underground forces.

Suddenly, after they had plodded painfully along for about half an hour, they heard voices and dogs barking. Perhaps the Japs were already on their trail! Hurriedly they dived into some bushes. But they saw nothing of the searchers, and, after the noise had died away, they pressed on again.

However, it soon became obvious that the wounded were in such a bad condition that they needed medical attention. The party decided to seek help from the local villagers.

A few minutes afterwards they heard voices once more, and again they hid in the bushes. Presently, they saw men approaching. Peering cautiously through the leaves, they noticed the Orientals wore civilian-type clothing and that one man had on a straw hat. The searchers looked like Thai villagers but they might be Japs. The evaders could not be sure.

Taking a big risk, injured Major Gildee walked forward. The rest of the party remained screened behind the bushes. Then, after watching him contact the Orientals, they saw him wave them forward. They came out of their hiding-place and followed the Thais to their village, Ta-Klee. There they were well treated.

That afternoon, the villagers went back for Naparolski, whom the evaders had had to leave behind because he was in so much pain. He was dead when the Thais found him.

*

Next morning Copley had a shock when he awoke. Staring bleary-eyed out of his bamboo hut, he was startled to see a party of mounted men, in uniform, galloping round the village.

'The Japs are here!' Curly yelled, rousing the others. Immediately panic broke out; though, in their pitiably injured condition, there was little they could have done to defend themselves.

The leading horseman trotted up to their hut and stared in. He had protruding yellow teeth, slanting eyes, and Oriental-style uniform. He looked like a true son of Nippon.

But then, to everyone's surprise, the leader warned them, in gestures and pidgin English, that a Japanese patrol was on its way in and that the crashed airmen must leave the village immediately. The horseman, it turned out, was a Thai police lieutenant who had come to help them.

The airmen were taken by bullock carts, which were essential to carry the wounded, to a stream outside the village. There they hid all day. Then, during the following two nights, they travelled on by bullock cart, escorted by the Thai police. Eventually they came to a stretch of water.

As he sat staring out across the river, Curly wondered what was to become of them. They hadn't a clue where they were going and they didn't know why the police were helping them. He tackled the police lieutenant. But the officer merely grinned reassuringly and said: 'Not worry. You all right.' The evaders were even more puzzled, but resigned themselves to leaving their fate in the hands of the Thai police.

Taken by boat to the house of Captain Rian Pacheetool, police captain of the province of Nakorn-Sawarn, the evaders learned that they now had to cross a railway line constantly patrolled by Jap guards.

As the party crouched in some bushes near the railway track, they watched breathlessly as the police captain crept cautiously up the embankment. He was checking if the coast was clear. Then they saw him beckon. The first evader slipped silently across the track. At length it was Curly Copley's turn to go across.

Noiselessly, Curly slung one arm around wounded Mac McCarthy, while Ramsey Roe supported Mac from the other side. Crouching low to remain unseen, Copley and Roe dragged the helpless Mac up the embankment.

Curly looked anxiously up and down the track as he nipped across the gleaming metals. Armed Japanese guards, he knew, were patrolling within a few hundred yards. But he saw no one. Then, his heart still pounding wildly, he hopped down to the river bank on the other side, the whole time dragging Mac with him.

There the party boarded a motor launch in which they chugged down-river for one-and-a-half cramped days. Sometimes the heat became so unbearable that the rush mats hiding them from prying eyes had to be rolled up. Frequently, the police captain yelled a sudden warning as a Japanese craft came near, and they had to bob down their heads, hoping they would not be seen. The slightest mishap would have given them away.

The following day the evaders reached Bangkok. There they were left tied up to a jetty for two hours. A huge crowd of Orientals stared at them from the quayside, and it was obvious from the evaders' colouring, of course, that they were Europeans. Worse, they knew that Bangkok was occupied by the Japs.

One yellow-skinned man kept eyeing them continuously. He was an evil-looking fellow who wore a military-style green uniform. He appeared the epitome of a Jap soldier. He stared at them for a whole hour, giving the boys the jitters. But he did nothing.

Eventually, to the evaders' enormous relief, an ancient bus rolled up. The airmen piled on board, then drove through the main streets of Jap-occupied Bangkok. It was broad daylight and, as the rush mats at the side of the bus flapped in the breeze, Copley saw scores of Jap soldiers, wearing their characteristic long peaked caps and puttees up to the knees, walking in the streets. They were so close that Copley could almost have put out his hand and touched them.

The evaders soon arrived at Thai Police Headquarters where, that night, they went to bed in a long cell-like dormitory. Though their beds were solid boards, covered only with straw mats, they fell asleep within a matter of minutes.

Suddenly, in the early hours of the morning, Curly

felt a hand shaking him. Waking up with a start, he blinked bewilderedly at the yellow beam of a torch shining into his face. He tried to move his lips, but a firm hand was clamped over his mouth to stop him speaking. And then, from out of the shadows, he heard his skipper, Flying Officer Smith, whisper in his ear: 'Come with me.'

*

Completely mystified, Curly slipped off his bed and padded over to three dark figures standing outside the beam of light in a comer. One of the three Curly recognized as Major Gildee, but the other two men he had never seen before. And then he was staggered to hear Smithy, after introducing him as his rear-gunner, add: 'Meet Dick and Howard.'

To Copley's utter astonishment, one of the strangers then reached over from the shadows, and, in a strong American accent, said: 'Hello Curly. Have a drink.' A moment later, the stranger thrust a bottle of Johnnie Walker into Copley's hands and offered him a packet of Camels.

The sudden shock of this surprising encounter shook Curly to the core. A minute ago, all he had to hope for, at the very best, was internment by the Thais for the rest of the war – even if he managed to escape falling into the hands of the Japs. Now, he found himself unexpectedly among friends who could obviously help him, and freedom was practically within his grasp. This sudden change of fortune was almost more than Curly could believe.

It was then, for the first time since the prang, that Copley learned, in quick whispered explanations from Smithy, the whole astonishing set-up.

The two American officers whom Curly had met, Major Dick Greenlee, and Captain Howard Palmer, were American Office of Strategic Services (OSS) secret agents. Operating from a secret headquarters in the heart of Jap-occupied Bangkok, with 15,000 Jap troops a stone's-throw away, they were working hand-in-glove with the Free Thais. These underground forces included members of the Thai police, which explained why the police had been so helpful to the evaders.

Astoundingly, the Regent of Thailand himself was head of the Free Thai underground movement. Thailand was, of course, technically at war with the Allies. Yet, while the Regent officially assisted his Japanese 'allies' in their struggle against Britain and America, in fact he was passing top-secret military intelligence to the Allies and was preparing the Thai underground forces for a projected possible revolt to drive out the Japs. His motive for double-crossing the Japanese was that he feared a stab in the back from them.

The evading airmen, Copley quickly realized, had stumbled on a secret plot of the most enormous magnitude. That was why it was vital the Japs should be prevented from finding out that Americans were on board the crashed kite. If the Japs had got wind of the true purpose of the Liberator's secret mission, the whole sensational underground plot would have come tumbling about the Free Thais' ears.

Understandably, the shooting-down of the Liberator had given the OSS men in Bangkok a colossal headache. Immediately, the Thai Chief of Police had sent out a police patrol to pick up the crew. The patrol had been ordered to prevent, at all costs, the airmen falling into Japanese hands. A patrol had also been dispatched by the Japanese. The Jap patrol had, in fact, searched the first village half an hour after the evaders had left – but they had later been ambushed by the Thai police and all the bodies buried.

The American members of the crew were now being spirited away to keep their presence secret from the Japs. The Thais, as official 'allies', of course had to inform the Japs about all airmen they interned and this included the rest of the Liberator's crew. But the remaining RAF men could safely be left in Thai hands; for, with the skipper gone and the navigator dead, the gunners and Wops could tell their Jap interrogators that all they knew about the mission was routine duties.

Timber Woods was awakened and told the score. He was instructed to convince the Japs that, as far as he knew, the Liberator had been on a meteorological flight. The OSS officers, he was also informed, would keep tabs on the rest of the crew in the Thai internment camp and get them out at the earliest opportunity.

The Americans at OSS headquarters in Bangkok, Copley now learned, could cope with one more British airman in addition to Smithy. So Curly now found himself taken along there with the American officers. He was selected, rather than any of the others, because of his long service overseas.

At about midnight on their sixth day in the secret headquarters, Copley and Smith, together with several other escapers who had joined them, piled into a battered old bus to begin their journey home. To his horror, Copley found that they had gone only a few yards when the ancient jalopy started back-firing furiously. The driver kept getting out, tinkering under the bonnet and yelling loudly to the police escort in Thai. Then he would get in, let in the clutch . . . and further tremendous bangs would echo through the still night air.

Sitting in the back, with a tommy-gun gripped between his knees, surrounded by tough Thai policemen also heavily armed, Copley spent several nerve-racking hours expecting a Jap patrol to challenge them at any minute. They were in a main street of Bangkok, in the early hours of the morning, and the police escort, Copley knew, were fully prepared to fight their way out if surprised by the Japs. Eventually, however, the party got back to Free Thai headquarters without mishap.

The following night, taking a spare bus this time, just in case, they drove out of Bangkok and reached Ban-Pe airfield. Copley took off at dawn in a Taylorcraft-type small cabin plane, while Smith went in another machine. The flight was scheduled to last about two hours. But, after Copley's Taylorcraft had been airborne for quite a number of hours, suddenly the Thai pilot made hopeless signs at the fuel gauge, which indicated empty; gestured frantically at his map; and looked desperately down at the jungle. He was lost!

A few minutes later, a small airstrip came into view, and the young pilot indicated that he was going to land.

'Japanese?' someone asked.

'Thai-Japanese,' replied the pilot. The airfield below was under joint Thai and Japanese control. Almost certainly the Japs would not permit a strange aircraft to land without investigating. It looked as if the game was up!

The Taylorcraft landed, and the pilot yelled to a mechanic for fuel. Then, to his dismay, Copley saw the mechanic returning with a 45-gallon drum of petrol, together with a hand-pump.

Refuelling would obviously take ages – and a Japanese patrol was likely to roll up at any minute.

Suddenly, the other Taylorcraft landed. Its pilot, an elderly, grizzled Thai, taxied over and called out with a reassuring grin:

'My friend lost. You come with me.'

They all hopped out into the other kite; and, within twenty minutes, they landed at the airstrip which they had originally been seeking.

Next day, a No 357 Squadron Dakota lobbed in for them, and Copley and Smith arrived back in India less than three weeks after they had been shot down. The other members of the crew after being interned by the Thais, were spirited out to freedom about two months later.

The skipper, Flying Officer Harry Smith, was subsequently awarded a DFC for the magnificent way in which he crash-landed the Liberator on dead-stick in spite of serious injuries.

Sometimes, the alternative to escape was death. Towards the end of the war, the Germans selected hostages from among prisoners of war, making it clear that the latter could be shot at any time by way of 'reprisals'. *One such hostage was Leading Aircraft-man Peter Shelton, who, aged twenty-three was captured in August 1942 while on Combined Operations during the tragic Dieppe landings. He spent a year in prison hospitals, suffering from shell shock. By posing as a pilot for some time, he was able to escape Hitler's infamous 'Commando Order' which stated that all those captured in any commando operation were to be executed. The spring of 1945 found him in an emaciated state in* Stalag Luft VI *– with the prospect of execution looming larger than ever.*

10

I Gambled with Death – and Won

Escape! My whole existence revolved round that word. It was the magic key that locked my sanity from straying. Escaping from the notorious *Stalag Luft* VI had become a challenge to me.

It was March 1945. Hourly, Allied aircraft droned overhead to pound nearby Hanover. The Liberation of Europe was well under way. But our release seemed as remote as the moon.

Ours was a punishment-camp, from which men could be selected for the mass shootings that the Nazis made infamous. We had no bedding, no decent food, no proper medical attention, no fires. Inmates died like flies – and were buried with as scant ceremony. For always there were others to replace them. Sometimes, I wondered whether we were caged in a clearing house for the crematoriums.

That's why escape became so vital. Ten thousand prisoners spent every waking moment dreaming of nothing else. I had been in the camp nine months – but had still not worked out a sound plan.

Chronic ill-health made tunnelling a dangerous risk. Crack-shot guards, probing searchlights and starved wolf hounds made it impossible to go through the thickly coiled barbed wire. The only sure way of leaving *Stalag Luft* VI was as a corpse . . .

I had already spent three years in enemy prison camps – and had become hardened to the routine; the boredom, the propaganda, the surly guards who often used their bayonets for prodding anything and anybody. We retaliated by go-slow methods. It was pantomime that wasn't funny. The days were long, the nights lonely. Prison camp 'blues' attacked everybody . . . sometimes leading to suicide.

I had got used to staring at the ceiling, letting my thoughts range far beyond the barbed wire. But always the heavy tramping of jack-boots and the sniffling of hounds brought me back to reality . . . brought me back to thinking of escape.

By 1945, life in *Stalag Luft* VI was hell. We ate mangy cats, raw potato peelings, leaves, roots, swill – anything our bony hands could grasp. The guards were tougher, and more trigger-happy. The air was full of foreboding and rumours. We were to be transferred to badly bombed Hanover in an attempt to stop the RAF crushing it still further . . . we were to be mass exterminated as a reprisal for the hammering the Ruhr was getting. . . we were to be mowed down 'while attempting to escape' . . . death certificates were already prepared and endorsed to that effect!

The rumours grew! Escape was no longer an adventure – it was a dire necessity. Escape – or die, became our sole maxim.

One morning this was brought home to me. I had stood staring at a woman outside the barbed wire; she was the first woman I'd seen for three years. But staring at a German woman was a capital offence, a livid officer screamed. I was to be shot for my rashness!

But for some reason the sentence wasn't carried out at once. During my temporary reprieve came the long-awaited order; the whole camp was to move deeper into Germany. We were to be used as shields in a Nazi last-ditch effort to hold up the Allied advance.

In columns of 300 we started the long trek towards Berlin. Dysentery and malnutrition made progress a painful nightmare. Bullying guards added their own *hors d'oeuvre* of kicks and punches. No food was served, and we chewed grass and roots like the animals we were. Emotionless civilians eyed our pitiful condition with indifferent silence.

At dusk our 300 scurvy-ridden skeletons were crammed into a barn big enough to hold only a third as many as it did. Inside the barn were poultry, soon the air was full of strangled clucking and flying feathers. Cooked over a smouldering fire, the birds were delicious. While the others broiled the fowls, I milked the cow that shared the barn with us.

For two days we marched through the Ruhr. Things were getting desperate. The Germans refused to issue any rations, and promptly shot all lingerers. I had to escape now . . .

I put my plan up to three others. The four of us would make a break as one unit. Four would have more chance of surviving than one. They agreed.

That night we slept in another barn. The air was full of sour sweat and urine. Dysentery turned the barn into a communal toilet. Came the dawn – and the escape started. Dry-mouthed, we walked out into the open – to be met by a menacing semi-circle of Nazi Stormtroopers, tommyguns trained on the barn!

To turn back would arouse suspicion, and earn a bullet, and could end with the whole 300 being slaughtered. Our guards were trigger-happy. Struggling with our fears, we started gathering sticks to light a fire. The Germans glared at us – but did nothing. Gradually our search area for sticks widened. Now we were outside the deadly semicircle . . . and still we hadn't been stopped.

More prisoners were now in the yard: enjoying the weak sunshine, trying to take no notice of the Stormtroopers, or that we were now farther behind them. A quick glance at the Germans, and I signalled to the others to make a bolt for a nearby haystack. Any second, I expected to hear the crackle of gunfire, but nothing happened!

All that long day we shivered and sweated in the hay, knowing that discovery would mean death. Our grim game of hide-and-seek with the enemy had started. We would now be classed as spies.

Dozens of times, guards walked past the stack. Once came an ominous scratching at the hay. Wolf-hounds! We'd been spotted after all, and the Germans were gloating at the thought of their dogs ripping us to pieces in a few moments!

I was tempted to get up and plead for mercy. But fear paralysed my body. We all stopped breathing. The scratching came closer. Then a familiar-looking scaly foot stuck itself in my face. The scratching belonged to a hen! For a long time panic-sweat bubbled down our faces.

At dusk – after ridding ourselves of everything but essentials – we set off, guided by a button-sized compass, survival of repeated Gestapo searches. Our goal was Bremen – and the advancing Allies. We tried to forget that between us and freedom were countless thousands of ruthless enemy troops.

In a well-spaced-out crocodile, we struggled across muddy fields and ditches. The pace sorely sapped our limited stamina. But a dim, warning glow kept us on the move; frightening us into slow progress with the knowledge there was no turning back now.

The warning glow also alerted us to the presence of dogs. We'd heard the whining for some time, but had assumed it was the wind playing tricks. But now there was no mistaking the barking that came from behind. All the time it was getting closer . . .

Our trail had soon been picked up! Shortly, the dogs would close in, tearing, ripping, snarling. Perspiration trickled down our faces. Everything was forgotten in the menace of the hounds.

Just in front was a wood. Maybe there'd be some safety there; what sort we didn't know – or care. As long as it was safety. Blind panic ousted reason. We gained the trees – and had another shock. Hanging from the first was a corpse! A sober warning to the fate we could expect.

*

Suddenly, the steady throbbing of aircraft engines drowned the panic that jangled my nerves. One of our aircraft was flare-dropping. We were right in a target area!

In seconds, the landscape was day-bright. But the baying of the dogs had ceased. Probably the Germans had taken shelter for the raid that was to follow. It was a heaven-sent reprieve with the thumping of high explosives. It was sweet music in our ears.

We covered fifteen long and tired miles that night.

But still fate hadn't finished with us. Cold and hungry, our senses dimmed with the events of the past few hours, we didn't see the civilian before he sprang out on us.

His armband said he was a member of the dreaded SD – a vast espionage system which watched the private life of every German and became the sole intelligence agency for the Nazi Party. He questioned us in a high-pitched, angry voice. We surrounded him, and heaped English curses on his head. In the half-light we looked like French forced-labourers; my Paris cavalry coat heightened the illusion.

But things looked sticky. The German pointed at a nearby village, and indicated we were to go there. That was the last thing we would – or could – do. Suddenly, he broke away from us and ran towards the village. Unarmed, we could not stop him. But the alarm was out for us again!

Running until we were dropping, we came to a shallow stream. Realizing that dogs would join the pursuit, we waded upstream for some time, hoping that this would throw the hounds off the scent. It did – for though we heard the dogs howling, they never picked up the trail.

But we were now past our endurance. We would have to eat, rest and replan. By now the whole countryside would be alerted; we had become Aunt Sallys in a manhunt in which anybody could shy at us.

Blindly, we floundered on through the fog that suddenly enveloped the countryside: stumbling, tottering automatons, goaded on by that one phrase: escape – or die.

The fog lifted none too soon . . . and we saw a small wood. Quickly, we dug a shallow trench, settled down in it and covered ourselves over with brambles and bushes. It was like being in a grave.

We slept until late afternoon. Unkempt, unwashed, untidy – we looked like scarecrows. That night we crunched uncooked sugar beet. It tasted horrible. But I had long reached a compromise with my stomach. Anything that could be swallowed – was!

The meal over, we took stock of our position. We could no longer bank on undetection. Often we could hear dogs quartering the countryside. It reminded me of a hunt. We were the foxes.

But we could do nothing.

For two days we lay in that grave, too weak to move, praying to survive. Once a Typhoon nearly shot us up. The pilot must have thought the wood held German stores . . . his rockets sizzled and scorched uncomfortably close.

Later that day I looked out – and saw two SS guards, guns at the ready, literally on top of us. Fortunately, they were looking the other way. Hardly daring to breathe, we took it in turns to keep tabs on them through our meagre bramble cover.

For almost an hour we were forced to remain motionless in a cramped position. It was the longest hour I've ever spent. Luckily, there were no dogs about. Eventually the guards moved away across the fields . . . we had survived another narrow squeak!

Later that night we had an even closer shave. The shock of the SS men was just wearing off, when more footsteps were heard approaching. We lay completely still. The footsteps came closer. We stopped breathing. The steps stopped right next to us. For what seemed a century there was a pregnant silence. Then the steps slowly retreated. Either we'd been taken for corpses, or hadn't been seen.

This last shock evaporated our morale like rain water. One of us wanted to go back – and hope for the best. I pointed out that the 'best' would be a speedy rifle bullet. Nobody spoke. Then we all agreed it was better to press on.

It was broad daylight as we continued our perilous escapade through Germany. We kept clear of the transport-infested roads. But once we had to cross one – and ran straight into more trouble! A *Luftwaffe* officer spotted us. Unarmed, he high-tailed it down the road on his bicycle. Soon another search party was looking for us. But now we were getting used to being hunted . . .

Across more fields, more ditches, more woods, more streams – always we moved. We must have covered twenty-five killing miles that day. The pace was starting to tell. Prison-camp conditions were not conducive to cross-country treks.

Once, I heard my voice gabbling and mumbling – but I could do nothing to check it. I swallowed hard, and thought of cruder and more realistic things. Revenge! I prayed that some day I would get revenge for what I was suffering now. This desire obsessed me – but gave me the will to continue.

Thirst was our biggest problem. At sunset we raided a farm, and forced the farmer to bring water. He gave us a cup each. Angrily, we pointed at a well. In the end we gulped two buckets full between us. Water literally trickled out of our ears!

The aged farmer told us that the 'Amerikanos' were only seven kilometres down the road. Excited, we set off in a staggering, tottering group. Our marathon walk across the face of Nazi Germany was ending, we hoped.

But the 'Amerikanos' turned out to be an evacuated American PoW camp. Either the farmer had misunderstood us, or tried to trick us. But we were past caring now. Ahead was a fair-sized wood. Rest was all we wanted. Unthinking, we headed towards it.

Suddenly, we were surrounded by tommygun-armed SS men! The wood was an arsenal. I wanted to run, to scream, to do anything that would get me out of this unholy jam. But I did nothing. Then hate forced a smile to my sickly face – and guided me through the tommy-gunners! I'd learnt a few words of German

– mostly how to curse Allied airmen. I produced these with good effect. The SS men relaxed slightly, and the four of us walked away from them. In the half-light we had once again been mistaken for French labourers.

There were hundreds of Germans in the woods. Most were busy loading ammunition on to lorries, the rest were air-raid watchers. We walked through them, sweating like stokers. We increased our pace . . . the wood was cleared. But we couldn't go any farther. We had reached a dead end; a sheer drop tapered off from the trees.

Suddenly, somebody shouted from behind us. We were trapped.

Not one of us moved. Any second we expected that shout to be followed by gun shots. Then it dawned: nobody was bothering about us. The shout had been a warning that Allied aircraft had been spotted approaching the arsenal. In a few minutes we would probably be blasted out of existence!

Panic replaced fear. We had to get out of this wood – quickly. Throwing caution to the wind, we retraced our steps at a shuffling run. All round, Germans were high-tailing it for shelter. In the distance the roar of aircraft engines grew louder.

Suddenly, the wood was brightly lit. Pathfinders had pinpointed it. The flare spotlit the confusion that existed. Ammunition boxes were scattered around the trees. Half-loaded lorries lined the lee side of the trees. They would never be loaded now.

The whole countryside was aglow with flares. Tin-hatted ack-ack gunners were feverishly stoking shells into the slim barrels of their guns, ready for the search-lights to pick out a target for them.

Nobody was taking any notice of us, and in a last desperate burst we got clear of the trees. Some of the flares had died, leaving the ground in shadow again. But the roar of aircraft engines was deafening.

I looked up. The bomber stream was over the wood! But they passed overhead. For some reason they had not bombed the arsenal. My prayers had been answered.

Exhausted after our nerve-shattering ordeal, we spent the night in a spinney some distance from the arsenal. We must have looked a pitiful sight huddled together in the cold moonlight. We were all hungry and tired.

What was worse was the fact that my mind was starting to cloud over. Over and over again, my brain urged me to reach out for the food that lay just out of reach. There were plates of steaming sausages and mash, bottles of raw revitalizing whisky, lashings of steak and onions. All I had to do was reach out for it . . .

But it was leaves and twigs that my hands grabbed.

*

Next morning we resumed our slow march – passing through several German villages. They reminded me of the English hamlets I knew so well, but which now seemed part of another world.

Nobody made any attempt to stop us. Gradually our morale returned. After surviving the past few days, we felt we could survive anything.

Cocksure, we entered yet another village, and came to twin-forked roads. We took the left-hand one – and ended walking into a German billet. Rifles and equipment were scattered about the converted barn.

For a minute, I was tempted to arm the four of us. But commonsense told me that escaping prisoners captured armed would have no defence at all. Even the Geneva Convention wouldn't protect us . . . not that the Nazis took much notice of any rules of humane warfare.

Beating a hasty retreat, we ran into a small band of gas-masked soldiers, all armed. Nobody moved. Then the Germans brushed roughly past us. We had either been mistaken for villagers or forced labourers.

The strain on our nerves was starting to tell. We realized that our amazing run of luck couldn't hold out for ever.

Clear of the village, we sketched out a story to tell the Germans should we be challenged. It went something like this: 'We admit we are British PoWs. But we are *not* escaping. We all suffer from chronic dysentery, and have dropped out of our marching column. We are now trying to refind the column.'

Our poor health condition would help to authenticate this story. Our story word perfect, we resumed the trek.

Overhead, aircraft roared and winged their way at high speed: the RAF were playing their part in crushing the Nazi menace. The thunder of heavy guns echoed over the horizon . . . we were getting towards the front line.

Eventually we came to Bergen. Once it had been a small, unknown village. Then Hitler opened a concentration camp near there. He called it Belsen. But we didn't know we were at the doorstep of the world's infamous mass execution chamber . . .

After scouting round the outskirts of Bergen, we decided to hide-up in some nearby woods, less than a mile from the front gates of Belsen. It was in the trees that we met the four Russians – escapees from the concentration camp.

*

They were a terrible indictment of the horror of Belsen; hollow-eyed skeletons dressed in filthy rags, looking and acting like animals. The sight of them frightened me more than all our encounters with Germans.

But they were friendly enough, and in a short while we were trading tea for some potatoes they had.

Hardly had we started eating – than thirty heavily armed Storm troopers crashed the meal. Viciously, they lined us up. We were going to be shot out of hand!

Fear had been my companion for a long time. But he was nowhere to be seen now that the danger was greatest. My whole mind was void. Dimly, I became aware we were not to die – yet. With typical thoroughness, the Germans started searching us. Here was hope. Once they discovered our British PoW discs, we might be saved.

Then came trouble: the Russians were armed! Gleefully, the Germans yanked automatics and ammunition out of their rags. We were in a hell of a spot. Not even the discs could save us.

Then came rescue.

A German who spoke English approached us. We blubbered our story over to him. He took our side. The other Stormtroopers looked angry at being cheated of their sport. They vented their fury on the unfortunate Russians – kicking and punching them with savage abandon. Death would be a merciful release for them.

Our 'dysentery' story fooled the English-speaking German. He took us to the Bergen Military Hospital, a well-organized place, reputed to be protected from Allied bombing and shelling.

Here we were interrogated by a high-ranking officer. Clearly, he would have liked us to stay at the hospital (to be found looking after Allied prisoners when the war ended would no doubt be in his favour), but his orders were that we must be sent to Soltau, where there was a German check-point for dealing with all escapees.

I had an idea that the check-point would only be a cover for an execution yard.

Then came hope again. There was no transport. We would have to go to Soltau on foot. Now, there was more chance of escaping. Shuffling slowly – oh, so slowly – along we thought up means of fooling our solitary guard.

*

We had heard that the Allies were only five miles away; we could hear their artillery pounding the Germans into submission. It was galling having to be so close – and yet so far from freedom.

We persuaded our guard to go slower. Then we persuaded him to take to the lanes, pointing out that the main roads would soon be strafed by the RAF. Our plan was in progress.

We bribed the German with our remaining cigarettes . . . and walked slower and slower.

Eventually, we came to a small village, and gave the guard the slip. The village housed hundreds of forced labourers who had been left there by the retreating Germans. We mingled with them. The menace of Soltau was over.

As soon as the labourers heard we were British, they gave us a great welcome. Sumptuous banquets were held in our honour. It was bad for the dysentery – but we didn't care!

That night we slept in a barn, listening and watching

gun-tracer pattern the sky into fantastic shapes. The Germans were fighting a brave rearguard action. We wondered what our fate would be should they return to the village?

But late next day, Cromwell tanks poked their squat fronts over a nearby ridge, but didn't enter the village.

Behind them came troops. Then hand-picked suicidal SS troops entrenched in woods close-by opened fire. Soon the landscape was full of bloody fighting.

Once more freedom had been dangled before us – then withdrawn.

Determined to play our small part in the fighting, the four of us started shouting to the Germans to surrender. Over and over again we told them there was no point in fighting on. More Cromwell tanks approached the village – and lent strength to our arguments. I also hoped they wouldn't open fire on the buildings.

The Germans were undecided. Some stopped shooting. Our pleas were having effect. We shouted louder. To clinch the matter we hauled a white sheet up over the village. The firing on both sides ceased. The tanks rumbled to a standstill on the fringe of the village.

Laughing like fools, we ran towards them. A fresh-faced youth stuck his head out of a gun turret.

'Blimey! Brylcreem Boys,' he cracked. 'Trust the Army to save the RAF!'

I knew then it was all over. My gamble with death had paid off.

The flame that spurs prisoners of war to escape springs from varied sources. In the case of Christopher Portway, taken prisoner by the Waffen *SS at Caen in 1944, it was the memory of a Czech girl – Dana – whose family had sheltered and fed him during the gruelling 'death march' from* Stalag *VIIIB in Upper Silesia to Austria in the winter of 1944-5.*

This story tells of Portway's final and successful escape, during which he witnessed – often at uncomfortably close quarters – the death struggles of the once proud Wehrmacht *and the abasement of the German nation. Courage brought him through, and the determination that he would one day return to Czechoslovakia and claim the girl he had grown to love.*

11

Journey to Dana

The commandant's announcement of the continuance of the march was a severe blow, coming as it did at a time when life was tolerable and the war very obviously drawing to a close. With liberation almost in sight, we were to trudge back along those hard dusty roads, every step taking us farther and farther from our approaching liberators. But prisoners are accustomed to disappointments and when the number of unmentionable places to which all Germans were again consigned had been exhausted the more profitable task of making preparations for the move carried us all into a world of activity. Food having become the pivot of our existence, one of the biggest headaches that immediately presented itself was that of the transport and carriage of our precious food parcels. This was solved in numerous ways – more successfully by those required on the last work-shift, who returned to camp laden with hand-carts, perambulators and a whole variety of miscellaneous vehicles 'acquired' in the town. But even those in camp, remembering vividly the hunger of the march, contrived to rig up ingenious methods of transportation.

Gordon and I, however, were singularly unsuccessful in our efforts, and by afternoon were getting desperate, when the familiar wail of the Plattling air-raid sirens gave me an idea.

Immediately the compound began rapidly to empty, while the two guards moved towards the camp buildings. Running like a hare into the warehouse, I grabbed a food parcel from our store. Tucking this firmly under my arm, I dashed out again and, threading my way swiftly through the incoming tide of humanity made for the north-western corner of the compound. Climbing the wooden fence presented no great difficulty and within a matter of seconds I was striding purposefully towards the nearest hedgerows fighting the urge to run and the expectancy of a bullet from a still-watchful sentry. Once in the shadow of the green, budding foliage, I breathed freely again, and ventured on towards a small farmhouse that I had observed from the camp. It came to me suddenly that I had successfully escaped from my prison again, but to take advantage of the situation and attempt a break for freedom without Gordon just did not appeal to me. This chance would come later, I told myself; meanwhile

I had a job to do, and that was to procure a conveyance for our stores.

Five minutes' walk brought me to the farmhouse, and with the feeling that I was being watched from the latticed windows I strode unhesitatingly up to the shabby doorway, firmly ignoring the exasperated yappings of a little dog. Expecting a man, I was relieved when the owner of the house stood before me in answer to my knock – a small kindly woman holding back an inquisitive child. In halting German I put forward my request, offering her in exchange the contents of my parcel. Had this been a few months earlier, I should probably have been promptly sent about my business, if nothing worse, but times had now changed, and Germany was tottering, her people on the brink of starvation. Her swift perusal of the various tins and sweetmeats was purely a formality, her tired eyes having lit up at the first sign of the parcel. In a sudden torrent of English, tinged with a strong American accent, I was given to understand that the good woman had lived in New York for twelve years and heartily wished she was back. It was quite a struggle to turn the very one-sided conversation back into its more practical channels, and when at last the glories of Fifth Avenue had been aired to her satisfaction I was to learn that the only contrivance she could offer was a wheelbarrow. For this, and half a dozen eggs, I handed over my parcel, and with my barrow rolling triumphantly before me, hastily took my leave, returning to camp by way of the main gate as if I had been on a special job in the town.

During my absence new events had taken place in the camp, and Gordon, after admiring the barrow, shook me with the news that Plattling camp was to be evacuated that very evening – in spite of the fact that the commandant, his officers and some of our senior camp staff were reported to be in a drunken stupor. The truth of the former statement was born out a few hours later, when shouting guards in full marching order spewed forth from the guard-house to direct the evacuation. Carefully stowing our precious parcels, we waited outside the warehouse while the great assembly of handcarts and barrows, together with their owners, slowly formed. In the west the sun began to dip behind the clouds, softening the outlines of the jagged ruins of Plattling.

As we filed out of the main gate, flanked on either side by amused guards, and on to the eastbound road, so the hungry civilians of the neighbourhood descended like a flock of hovering vultures upon the evacuated camp. It was a sure sign of the turn of events to watch the proud members of the exalted Aryan race foraging for food in a British prison camp!

*

The first mile of that useless expedition proved to Gordon and myself that we had been sold a pup. My precious wheelbarrow quickly began to overcome our physical powers of endurance, its solitary wheel emitting a constant stream of oil-demanding squeaks, as if jeering at our depressing efforts. Like all normal wheelbarrows, it was a one-man-power vehicle, and though we took it in increasingly short turns to provide the motive power, it soon became evident that we were unfit for the task.

For five, six, eight and more miles the two of us staggered on, gradually being overtaken by our fellow-countrymen with more efficient means of trans- port. The evening wore on and the small road appeared endless. Jettisoning at least some of our cargo seemed the only alternative. Suddenly Gordon said, 'Let's get the hell out of this!' and with those words our last escape bid was born. This one, however was to be more haphazard than its predecessors, the general idea being simply to wait until darkness fell, choose a moment when a suitable house or hedgerow provided cover and, with the position of the guards checked, run with our load in one supreme effort to gain concealment whilst the column passed slowly by.

Darkness found us still struggling onwards, and it was whilst passing through the little village of Leyling that we decided the time had come to test our ill-planned scheme. A watery moon was on our side, providing just enough light for our convenience but not drenching the countryside in brilliance. Carefully we studied afresh the movements of the guards.

Beween each German was a gap of about twenty-five yards, but as the line stretched unevenly each side of the column, his nearest neighbour on the other flank was generally a good deal nearer. Edging up to a few yards behind a left-flank guard, we awaited a chance to go. If possible, we wanted a sharp right-hand bend in the road, around which the guard immediately behind us would not be able to see, whilst the bulk of the column would obstruct the right-hand flank-man's view. We got the right-hand bends all right, but unfortunately the cover nearby was either inadequate or entirely non-existent.

Time and time again we were on the verge of hurling ourselves forward, only to be baulked at the last fraction of a second by some unforeseen circumstances, such as the guard in front turning his head or flashing his torch. The column wound relentlessly forward.

With nerves taut with suspense I took over the barrow from Gordon, and, rounding a right-hand bend, a concrete water-tower standing some fifteen or twenty yards back from the road came into view. 'Now!' hissed Gordon, and lunged outwards away from the road. Not daring to look anywhere and blindly trusting Gordon's appreciation of the situation, I broke into a frantic run across the grass verge, over some clinging turf and straight into a bog. For several ghastly seconds the wet mushy soil clawed us to a halt, before sheer desperation flung us forward again towards the nearby tower. I knew we could not make it, however, and urging Gordon to do likewise, threw myself prostrate on the ground, burying my head into the damp moss. Behind us, the trudging feet continued without pause, and with a tingling sensation at the back of my neck I commenced to crawl slowly towards our goal, leaving the barrow, highly conspicuous, to its fate. Gordon reached the base of the tower first, but dashed out again, on observing a break in the column, to rescue our cargo. Seeing his intention, I rose, and together we hauled the precious barrow to safety behind the concrete buttress.

*

Breathing heavily, we sat huddled together on the damp grass. Voices mingling with the tramp of boots were clearly audible, some even recognizable. Casually I wondered whether we would meet any of our friends again.

We let the column get well out of earshot before venturing to move from our shelter and then only with great reluctance, for the physical and mental strain of the past few hours was taking its toll. Our immediate problem was to find a less conspicuous shelter farther from the roadway, in which to spend the remainder of the night.

Moving away from the silent village, we followed a tall thorn hedge for some hundreds of yards before coming to an open gateway inviting us into what appeared to be a large meadow. The darkness now became a severe handicap, and we were unable to avoid the numerous ruts and other pitfalls into which the two of us and the barrow kept falling. Jubilation soon gave way to frustration, and the lush green grass around us must have withered from the language that poured uncontrollably from our lips. Though swearing is supposed to get nobody anywhere, it managed to bring us to an isolated little pond entirely surrounded by sheltering bushes and forming the perfect hide. Into this leafy sanctuary we hauled our troublesome cargo and, with a crackling of twigs, settled down for a much-wanted sleep.

The cold frost of an April night was soon to join forces with the darkness, denying us even this comfort and before the ghostly light of dawn could tinge the heavens we were up and about, stamping and arm-swinging, in an effort to generate a little warmth. In between these early morning antics we hastily formed a plan of action, to be put into operation with the coming of daylight. With the lesson of night-time foot travel rammed home and the danger of day travel within the Fatherland itself most obvious, we decided to make this a 'static job'. This involved the finding and occupying of a remote and safe 'hide ' in which we could remain until the arrival of the Americans, which we knew could not be long delayed. In our shivering state movement seemed more desirable than simply lying low day and night, but eventually the 'static' view was accepted. The first thing was to find our new home, however – a problem in itself, and one that involved the vetoed movement. We decided to solve it at daybreak.

Lying down again after a particularly energetic burst of stamping, we drifted into long overdue slumber which was rudely broken by the noise of violently disturbed undergrowth and childish voices. It seemed to me that I had only slept a few minutes, but bright daylight met my startled gaze, whilst the sight of a bevy of interested young spectators took some time to register. Gordon, on becoming reasonably conscious, tried to shoo the crowd of schoolchildren away, resorting to bribery with an offering of half a chocolate bar, prized from one of the parcels on which we were lying. Many of the youngsters, however, had hardly seen chocolate in their lives, and immediately upon beholding this rare treasure went wild with delight. This was most definitely not the desired effect, and it took nearly fifteen minutes to persuade our audience that we were no relations of Santa Claus and that there was no more chocolate. Slowly they drifted off, but hardly had we commenced reloading our barrow when parents and other inquisitive adults began to arrive in ever-increasing numbers, informed of our presence, no doubt by their offspring. Looking around us in amazed perplexity, we learnt the reason for this sudden collection of humanity: our shaded pond lay directly against a large village, a fact that we had failed to note in the darkness!

With the last of the parcels stowed, I suddenly had an idea. Why not bargain with our tame spectators for a few more convenient means of conveyance – Whispering my scheme to Gordon, who agreed, we started the ball rolling in atrocious German, our first offer of a tin of butter mounting to cover the whole of the contents of one parcel. Visibly impressed by our offers, many potential buyers only declined because they possessed no suitable vehicles; and seeing that we had no intention of giving anything away the crowd slowly evaporated until finally one girl, a beautiful creature with jet-black hair and grey eyes, stood hovering longingly nearby. '*Bitte, Lebensmittel für meine Kinder,*' she pleaded, in a manner designed to melt the hardest heart; but captives have no hearts at all where food is concerned, and, though now the incident touches my conscience, we stubbornly ignored her requests. Both our gazes were riveted admiringly on her shapely legs as she disappeared towards the village. A sure sign that we were becoming human beings again!

It was definitely time to depart before less harmless elements of the population put in an appearance. Already most of the village knew of our presence, so we decided to continue our journey on through the narrow street, instead of back across the bumpy fields; then, once away, to take again to the open countryside. The sun was well up as we left our doubtful sanctuary.

Reaching the farther outskirts of the village, with

Gordon as barrow-pusher, my eye suddenly caught sight of a highly modern and streamlined perambulator standing alone and unattended outside a small house, a hundred yards ahead of us. Inspiration came in a flash, and I quickened my pace until level with the pram, made a quick survey up and down the road, then leapt for my prey. With hardly a glance at it, I grabbed the handle, and was about to pull the contrivance after me up the street when a sudden gurgle emerged from the depths of the interior. Frightened out of my wits, I looked back and perceived, to my consternation, the grinning face of a tiny baby nestling amongst the pillows in the pram. For a few seconds I hesitated, panic-stricken, then I swooped upon the little bundle, lifted it and bedclothes as gently as circumstances would allow, and deposited them hurriedly on the doorstep. The toddler seemed vastly amused at the joke and guffawed loudly, sending me and its late pram hurtling up the road and out of earshot. With our two vehicles trailing astern, we made tracks for the wide open spaces.

Fearing pursuit, we left the road at the first opportunity and turned into a convenient bridle track leading northwards. Behind a tall hedge some fifty yards from the road we halted to effect the transfer of parcels to our newly acquired conveyance. I was a bit doubtful about the ability of the small, fragile-looking wheels of the pram to bear the unaccustomed weight, but resolved not to jump fences before coming to them.

It was as I was putting this piece of logic to Gordon that we felt, rather than heard, a presence behind us. Turning together, we found ourselves looking straight at a German soldier, complete with steel helmet, standing three yards away. His eyes, full of curiosity, bored into us, whilst his hand rested nonchalantly on the butt of an outsize holstered pistol. My mouth seemed suddenly to dry up.

Gordon was the first to recover from this unpleasant shock, 'Guten Morgen' he muttered hesitatingly. 'Engländer?' asked our tormentor pleasantly, as if stray British prisoners were normally to be found in German hedgerows. 'Ja,' we both replied, trying to look unconcerned. Making no attempt to arrest or detain us, he launched into a monologue in passable English on the unjustness of the Hitler regime and all it stood for.

In spite of his apparently pro-English attitude, I felt that an explanation of our presence would not be amiss, and, his lecture delivered, I told him that we were awaiting the next prisoner column to come by, having fallen out through lameness from the first. Hardly a watertight excuse, but it seemed to do the trick.

Of his own accord, our warrior gave us a report of the frontline fighting and excited us with the news that the Americans were driving hard for the area in which we now stood. Apparently he belonged to a unit whose task it was to delay the advance and who were now occupying a large forest four miles along our bridle path. This information was quietly stored away, and, as tactfully as possible, we pumped him for more. Beyond the fact, however, that the usual persuasive bodies of the unpopular SS were attached to his unit for purposes of bolstering morale, no further useful results were obtained. He left us as suddenly as he had come.

Hurriedly completing our packing operations, and dumping our barrow, with no regrets, in a nearby ditch, we sallied forth once more along the path. Our intention was to branch off eastwards after a mile, and then to keep on until we found a suitable wood in which to set up camp, and there await liberation.

The sun shone brilliantly and bathed the thickly wooded Bavarian countryside in its glorious rays. It was difficult to believe that not far distant a defeated army was reeling backwards against the sledgehammer onslaught of thousands of men and machines of the Allied nations. In the hedgerows and trees, the birds of spring, that no man-made war could obliterate, were in their full glory. Only the song of the birds was dimmed by the roar of aero-engines that never ceased, a sound to which I had grown dangerously accustomed during the past month. No longer did I trouble to look up as hordes of fighters swept across the sky, though that very afternoon we were to nearly pay the penalty for carelessness in this respect.

Passing near a river, we were hailed by German soldiers bathing in the cold water. I would have liked to join them, but contented myself by waving to them instead, whilst Gordon was so bold as to shout encouragement to a hesitant diver on the opposite bank. Once out of their sight, we took time off for a snack.

Negotiating a wire fence, we continued eastwards across open grazing land, moving parallel with the forest. The going became more difficult here, and the pram was less manoeuvrable on the uneven ground, whilst a series of further fences did not improve matters. However, we progressed steadily, and by afternoon had put a respectable distance between ourselves and Leyling.

Gordon was reloading some of the parcels into the pram after the negotiation of a particularly awkward fence when, out of a clear blue sky, death came hurtling down upon us. Subconsciously I had heard the noise of a low-flying plane, but took little notice of it, as the pram was being slowly raised and lowered by our combined efforts across the wire obstacle. Suddenly the tune of the engine changed into a crescendo of screaming power that demanded instant attention. Glancing upwards I was astounded to see an American Thunderbolt hurtling straight at us, the sunlight glinting on its wings. My yell to Gordon was purely incidental, he having already spreadeagled himself behind a blade of grass, whilst the slight dip in the ground into which I had flung myself was little better. The expected burst of gunfire only had the effect of drawing us still closer to Mother Earth, and the thud of bullets into the green turf was plainly heard, but not seen, our faces being buried in the resisting dirt. It could have all lasted no more than a few seconds, but in such moments even seconds can hang suspended in timeless space. Venturing to raise my head, I watched our attacker climb steeply and disappear westwards.

Rising shakily, we examined the pram and discovered the worst. A half-inch calibre shell had smashed the left-hand rear wheel before entering the curved base of the bodywork. With Gordon muttering something about 'military objectives', I tried to collect my scattered thoughts and consider the next move.

A small wood some two hundred yards distant was to attract my immediate attention. From where we stood it looked adequate for our purpose, the undergrowth being thick enough to screen our movements and the wood itself being too small to be occupied by large forces of Germans. Perhaps the crowning factor that dispelled any doubts was that it was the only small wood within sight.

It took us thirty minutes and half a dozen journeys, to convey our parcels, baggage and damaged pram to the leafy privacy of our chance-found home. A wire fence surrounded part of the wood – advantageous in the interests of security, but a decided nuisance during that half hour. The results of a reconnaissance by Gordon showed that our water supply was ensured by the presence of a small stream running along the bottom of a deep ditch on the northern flank of the wood.

Once safely installed amongst the trees, we set to work to construct a shelter for ourselves out of sticks and foliage, taking care to blend it with the surroundings in case of unwelcome visitations. Our parcels we placed in four rows on the ground, forming a dry base on which to sprinkle the softest foliage possible. Over this we built a skeleton of stout sticks, between which to intertwine lengths of vegetation. By nightfall we had completed a satisfactory though hardly rainproof hut, the finishing touches of which we proposed to do on the morrow. Between building operations we found time to make a small fire, which eventually persuaded a Klim-tin of water to boil, and under a darkening sky we sat down to enjoy a well-earned meal. In spite of bitter-tasting tea, caused probably by the semi-stagnant water, we did ourselves proud with the aid of a tin of bully-beef, Canadian biscuits, cheese, jam and some German *Knackebrot*, which for the last week at Plattling had become a substitute for bread. Finally, feeling well satisfied with life, we crawled on to our foliage-topped cardboard bed and pulled our single greatcoat over us. The last sound I heard was an owl hooting eerily in the darkness.

*

We remained in that wood for three further days and nights. Air activity continued overhead unabated, but the sound which first caught our ears and attention and held us spell-bound on the second morning was the rumble of distant gunfire. At first it was so faint that we dared not believe our senses, but gradually it increased in volume during the day until we needed no further confirmation. Once before we had listened to this mighty symphony of liberation and had heard it fade away from us. This time we were determined to await the grand finale.

With the passing of the first excitement, the long hours of waiting became intolerable. With our nerves on edge, we bickered all day between ourselves, flying into raging tempers at the slightest provocation. Rationing of food caused most trouble, Gordon wanting to devour large quantities at every meal, whilst I was for holding back in case of a prolonged stay. Many times our squabbles turned to blows, but each outburst died as fast as it began, and within seconds we would be laughing at our stupidity.

The second night brought a steady downpour of rain. Trees sheltered us for a short time, but then water steadily began seeping through our clothes. Next morning I discovered that in my sleep I had instinctively burrowed under Gordon's body, thus sheltering my own. Gordon discovered this as well, which resulted in further outbreaks of civil war!

Sometimes the rumble of artillery would die away leaving us in very depths of despair. Then the wind would change and salvo after salvo vibrated through the air. In efforts to pass the time we drank innumerable tins of dubious tea and coffee, but attempts to sleep away the hours were quite hopeless. At such moments, however, my thoughts would secretly linger upon the girl I had left behind in the little village of Kralovice. For the first time in my life I had fallen in love, although I should have laughed at the idea had anyone told me so. Vague plans for returning after the war were already astir within me, jostling for room with the main ambition to get safely home. Then an extra-violent burst of gunfire would transfer me back to the present, bringing us both to our feet in scrambling confusion.

The afternoon of the second day brought us a surprise visit from two Polish woodcutters. We saw them approach our hide and lay quiet, with the hope of not attracting their attention. However, the men came so close that they could hardly avoid seeing us, and when this occurred it was plain that they were more frightened. An American cigarette calmed their fears, and we parted the best of friends – they with a packet of 'Lucky Strikes', we with a replenished store of matches and information regarding a nearby herd of cows, which promised supplies of fresh milk. Gordon could not wait for morning and proceeded straightaway to the herd, which was grazing in the meadow bordering the eastern end of the wood. Within a quarter of an hour he was back empty-handed and most dejected. According to him, 'the damned things had all dried up!'

Our third night passed without special incident, but it was the noise of artillery fire that woke us. The tide of battle had surged forward suddenly during the hours of darkness, and the guns of both sides were perceptibly nearer; so much so that we could distinguish individual explosions. Excitement gripped us again as we crawled hurriedly from our shelter, but though we carefully scanned the horizon, nothing was to be seen.

In spite of a fine dawn, rain began falling about eight o'clock which, besides being unpleasant, made the lighting of fires none too easy. Whilst engaged in searching for dry wood near the ditch which was our water supply, we were taken by surprise with the arrival on the scene of two German soldiers carrying wireless equipment. Too late to dodge out of sight, we continued our task, and the two men, eyeing us curiously, passed by, walking steadily alongside the wood. Sensing danger, we resolved to play safe for the remainder of the day, and, a luke-warm cup of tea tucked away inside us, we extinguished our smouldering fire and sat tight in our shelter.

Time passed slowly as we lay in silence, listening to the music of the guns ever growing in volume. Each of us dreamed our dreams of freedom and probed into the future. Soon the nightmare would be over. 'Look!' hissed Gordon, breaking our twin trains of thought. Following his outstretched arm, my eyes swept across the open fields, to light upon a road of which we had no knowledge before. Doubtless we should not have seen it at all had not columns of German transport pouring eastwards along it drawn our attention. Though a mile away, we could plainly see lorries, guns and occasional tanks grinding steadily back to some last-ditch defence line, whilst intermingled with the endless line of vehicles exhausted grey-clad figures staggered wearily. Already we had seen the German army in desperate retreat from the Russians in the frozen wastes of Poland; now, on the soil of their own doomed country, we were witnessing the final death struggles of the bleeding *Wehrmacht*.

I have never really believed in mental telepathy, but I certainly came near it when within minutes of my remarking that the crowded road ahead would make an excellent target, a salvo of shells screamed urgently overhead and exploded bluntly in the distance. Further salvoes followed, and we could plainly pick out the dull thuds beforehand as the guns opened up to the west of us. Apparently an American battery had managed to move during the night with the object of speeding Jerry on his way and was now getting into its stride. Soon other batteries joined in, and the din became frightening.

Prudently moving nearer to our partly filled ditch, we debated the question of making our way towards the American lines. To do so, however, meant passing through the German line – an operation that demanded extreme care, even in the present situation – and finally it was decided to remain in our comparatively safe and camouflaged position.

All day the firing continued, and during the late afternoon heavy mortars joined the party, lobbing their shells ineffectively into the open meadows around the wood. We watched the spouts of turf and smoke with considerable concern. In comparison, evening brought a lull in proceedings, and we thankfully took the chance to light a small fire on which to brew some tea. By this time the distant road was empty and an uncanny hush settled over the waiting countryside. Not a breath of wind disturbed the new green leaves, and no bird sang amidst the silent trees. I shivered slightly as I nursed the fire.

Gordon, too, must have sensed the evil in the air, for he pleaded suddenly for a small feast of celebration on what we hoped would be our last night as captives. Relenting my enforced rationing rules, and being chief cook, I concocted a pudding made from French condensed milk, Canadian raisins, broken biscuits and sugar, which we devoured for our evening meal. Ten minutes later we were both violently sick and crawled to bed in a state of utter misery.

*

We found little sleep that night, though finally fatigue produced an uneasy slumber. Awakening to the unmistakable harsh rattle of machine-guns, it took us some moments to recollect that there was a war going on, then we were out of our shelter in a flash and moving swiftly to our uncomfortable ditch and vantage point. There was nothing to see in the early morning light as we peered eagerly westwards, trying to penetrate the mist, which lay blanket-like a foot from the ground; but of sound there was plenty. The firing seemed to come from the distant forest, and I could plainly distinguish the rapid rate of fire of German *Spandaus* from the heavier-calibre guns of the Americans. Gordon swore that he could hear the squeaky rumble of tank tracks, and, as after events were to prove, he was probably right. There is nothing more exasperating than being mixed up in a battle but seeing or knowing nothing, whilst being unable to take part in it is the last straw.

A loud double crash, followed by the whine of shell splinters, sent us clawing our way into the wet ditch. Two shells had burst on the eastern border of the wood and the situation was becoming definitely unhealthy. In spite of our hasty entry we managed to keep our feet dry clinging on to the banks of the ditch and lying lengthways a few inches from the surface of the water. In this eccentric position we remained for ten minutes, whilst a further series of explosions vibrated around us.

In the lull that followed I started to draw myself out of the ditch, when voices in German arrested my movements. Looking beyond our hut, I was horrified to see three wild-eyed and mud-splashed storm-troopers entering our sanctuary bearing between them a heavy *Spandau* mounted on a tripod. Whispering to Gordon to remain silent, I watched them place the gun in position, its wicked barrel nosing out from behind a tree. Clear memories of last-ditch stands by SS fanatics in Normandy, and of the grim holocaust of fire they drew before their extinction, flitted through my mind. The additional danger of being discovered by them was also not to be overlooked, and who could blame them for shooting us, in the circumstances? Together we lay and watched.

I noticed, shortly, that our unwelcome visitors appeared to be in difficulties with their ammunition clips, and one of them began hurriedly to strip the breech mechanism, loudly cursing its maker as well as his own. Whilst thus engaged, Gordon and I started to worm our way backwards along the ditch with the intention of getting as far away as possible from the do-or-die trio before the fun started.

We got no more than two yards, however, before the lull ended with more shattering explosions near the wood. These came in rapid succession, chasing each other playfully, the stick ending some two hundred yards from our position. Mortar bombs then took up the chorus, their sharp reports magnified by a hollow echo. This was quite enough for the intrepid machine-gunners, who suddenly decided that there was more future in doing than dying, grabbed up the immobilized *Spandau*, together with its odd bits and pieces, and retired in undignified haste to the southern border of the wood, where they took to the fields and disappeared from view.

Giving them three minutes' start, we climbed stiffly out of our trench and followed their tracks to the edge of the wood, where we ascertained that their departure was permanent. The firing had died down again and only the spasmodic growl of distant gunfire disturbed the early morning peace.

'A whisky and soda would go down all right now,' observed Gordon, and looking at him, I was inclined to agree. My bleary-eyed, unshaven and filthy companion was but a reflection of my own untidy self, whilst our tattered clothes would have shamed a scarecrow.

A little later we observed that, a hundred yards across the meadow, our herd of cows were being milked by a determined local, stolidly ignoring the battle that was being fought in the vicinity. We joined him hesitatingly, and, perhaps guessing our identity, he commenced gesticulating wildly in a westerly direction. At the same time he uncorked a stream of words spoken in a totally unrecognizable Bavarian dialect and in which two words – 'Americano Panzer' – predominated. Eventually, after repeated efforts, we were given to understand that American tanks had halted half a mile from our wood and were only hidden from view by a slight rise in the ground. Incredulous, but unwilling to disbelieve the statement, we dashed off, forgetting even to sample the white nectar frothing richly in the pails. Crossing the two fields at a steady run, we entered a small belt of trees and then, more cautiously, advanced up the grass rise. With our hearts thumping from exhaustion and excitement, we reached the top and beheld a sight that was infinitely more wonderful than any other I have gazed at in my life.

Some half-dozen grubby Sherman tanks, together with a few attendant half-track vehicles, nestled snugly in a small leafy clearing. Each bore on its side the white star of the Allied Expeditionary Force. Grouped around the tanks were parties of men in a motley of unmilitary clothing, but with the unmistakable American steel helmet perched nonchalantly on their heads. Three of them were cooking breakfast.

Hardly daring to believe our eyes, we advanced steadily towards our liberators, but scarcely had we taken ten steps when a shot rang out and a bullet whistled high overhead. We stopped, momentarily perplexed, before the realization dawned on us that in our present sorry state we were liable to be taken for anyone, including the enemy. Raising our hands high in the air, we yelled in unison, 'British prisoners of war! Don't shoot!', and waited for something to happen.

From our flanks, three heavily armed Americans drew in on us, their eyes cold with suspicion, and their automatic rifles pointing steadily at our stomachs. Upon their reaching speaking distance, we repeated our brief speech of introduction. Whilst two kept us covered, the third stepped forward and efficiently frisked us for concealed weapons. 'OK, fellows,' drawled our searcher, and grinned an expressive welcome. The two automatic rifles were suddenly withdrawn out of sight.

'I guess you're hungry,' said someone, as we joined the nearest group of smiling soldiers, and without further ado he passed us three fried eggs on the whitest slice of bread I could ever remember seeing. About my ninth egg I suddenly found that I knew what that often misused word 'freedom' meant.

*

In 1948, after a lengthy battle to obtain permission from the Czech authorities, Christopher Portway returned to Czechoslovakia and married his Dana. It was a short-lived happiness. After only a few months, their marriage – tormented by fears for the safety of Dana's family at the hands of the Communists and her own knowledge that she could never leave them to go to England – came to an end.

Acknowledgements

The stories in this collection have been taken from the various sources listed below and we should like to thank the publishers for giving us permission to reprint extracts from their publications.

Escape from Corregidor by Edgar D. Whitcomb; Allan Wingate (Publishers) Ltd.

The One That Got Away by K. Burt and J. Leasor; Collins, Publishers.

Escaper Extraordinary, RAF Flying Review.

Farewell Campo 12 by James Hargest; Michael Joseph Ltd.

The Big Break-Out, Wide World Magazine.

Boldness Be My Friend by Richard Pape; Paul Elek Limited.

Romanian Adventure from *P.O.W.* by Douglas Collins; Robert Hale Ltd.

Single to Rome by Wing Commander E. Garrad-Cole;
Allan Wingate (Publishers) Ltd.

Fugitives in Siam, RAF Flying Review.

I Gambled With Death, RAF Flying Review.

Journey to Dana by Christopher Portway; William Kimber
& Co. Limited.

ENDEAVOUR INK

Endeavour Ink is an imprint of Endeavour Press.

If you enjoyed *When Freedom Calls* check out
Endeavour Press's eBooks here:
www.endeavourpress.com

For weekly updates on our free and discounted eBooks sign up
to our newsletter:
www.endeavourpress.com

Follow us on Twitter:
@EndeavourPress